Walk in my Presence 2

Nicholas Hutchinson FSC

Matthew James Publishing Ltd

Also available by the same author:

Walk in My Presence 1 (2002)

– 30 Prayer Services

1 898366 60 8 – Walk in My Presence 1

Praying Each Day of the Year (1997-1998)

– a 3 volume series that offers a reflection and prayer specific to the anniversaries of events.

1 898366 30 6 – Volume 1: (January to April)

1 898366 31 4 – Volume 2: (May to August)

1 898366 32 2 – Volume 3: (September to December)

Lord, Teach us to Pray (1999)

– a 50 day course of personal prayer, exploring various ways of praying through creative use of Scripture and imagery.

1 898366 65 9 – Lord, Teach us to Pray

Published by
Matthew James Publishing Ltd,
19 Wellington Close,
Chelmsford, Essex CM1 2EE

ISBN 1 898366 76 4

First published 2002

Cover design by Peter Robb
Typeset by Linda East
Printed by J W Arrowsmith, Bristol

Dedicated to the memory of
Brother Edwin Bannon, FSC
(1917-2001)
who inspired and encouraged many
to touch the hearts and minds
of people of all ages

Contents

Foreword

The vivid and evocative imagery of *'walking with God'* is first encountered in the Book of Genesis. There we read that figures such as Abraham and Joseph *'walked with God'*[1], and God makes a promise to Eli: *"Your House... will walk in my presence for ever."*[2]

In a poetic way the psalms describe our relationship as *'walking in the presence of God'*[3] and we pray: *'Lord, teach me how to walk beside you faithfully'*[4]. These words are particularly poignant as a new day begins, and we ask that our eyes be opened to recognise the Risen Jesus, as happened to the two frightened disciples whose world had collapsed around them[5]. Jesus joined them and walked by their side but, at first, something prevented them from recognising him. As their eyes were opened, much fell into place and they knew that all manner of thing would be well. Their hearts were on fire as Jesus engaged them in conversation on the road and explained the scriptures to them.

For many Christians this remains one of the most prayed-over passages in the Gospels. The disciples' two-hour walk of discovery from Jerusalem to the village of Emmaus became the summit of their lifetime of exploring. It was as though they had arrived where they had started and knew the place for the first time[6]. That journey mirrors our searching each day with our own *'joys and hopes, and grief and anxiety... in our pilgrimage towards the Father's kingdom'*[7].

In that spirit, may all of us who use this book pray for one another and grow in compassion as companions who are sharing the same journey – that of 'the pilgrim people of God'[8] – knowing that, if we have eyes to see, we can discover that *'Earth's crammed with heaven and every bush is afire with God'*[9].

> **Brother Jesus,**
>   **your presence is interwoven**
>   **throughout each day of our lives.**
> **As we journey with our fellow pilgrims,**
>   **touch our hearts and open our eyes**
>   **that we may recognise you**
>   **walking beside us.**
> **Lead us to live in such a way**
>   **that we discover you**
>   **in the quietness and in the spaces,**
>   **as well as in the busyness**
>   **of our lives each day.**
> **Continue to call us your friends**
>   **and accompany us**
>   **to where we shall see our Father, face to face.**
> **Amen.**

---

1 – Gen 5[22], 6[9], 24[40], 48[15]; **2** – 1 Sam 2[30]; **3** – Ps 11[9]; **4** – Ps 56[13], 86[11]; **5** – Lk 24[13-35];
6 – cf. T.S. Eliot: *Little Gidding* V; **7** – Vatican II: Gaudium et Spes, 1; **8** – Vatican II: Lumen Gentium, 68;
9 – Elizabeth Barrett Browning: Aurora Leigh, bk. 7, l. 821

Reading

Cardinal Jean-Marie Lustiger

I delight in being able to dip my hand into a basin of holy water – beautiful, pure and fresh. It calls to mind baptismal water and the Easter Watch. Then I do not only make the Sign of the Cross *"in the name of the Father, and of the Son, and of the Holy Spirit"* but, by touching my head and chest with this water, I can recall the wealth of its symbolism which gives my life its grandeur: the first water of Creation over which the Spirit of God moved; the water of the Red Sea crossed by the Hebrews chosen to enter into a Covenant with God; the water of the River Jordan on the threshold of the Promised Land; the water of baptism; the water of tears which wash away our sins; living water that God causes to well up in us like a spring gushing forth from the Spirit.

So, when we get up in the morning, we can pray very simply: *"In the name of the Father, and of the Son, and of the Holy Spirit."*

Prayer

Peter de Rosa

1   Father, you contain within yourself the waters of life,
    and everyone who thirsts
    must come to you to drink.

2   The Psalmist wrote passionately:
    *"As the deer longs for running streams,
    so my soul is longing for you, my God.
    My soul is thirsting for God, the living God.
    When will I be allowed to see the face of God?"*

3   Again he says with equal ardour:
    *"O God, you are my God, I long for you;
    my soul is thirsting for you.
    My body is panting for you
    as in a dry, weary land without water"*…

4   On a hot midday at the well of Samaria,
    Jesus said to the woman drawing from the well:
    *"Everyone who drinks of this water will thirst again,
    but whoever drinks of the water I will give
    will never thirst.*

Introduction

This second volume of *Walk In My Presence* is of 32 prayer services appropriate for use in the seasons of the Church's Year. Most can also be used well at other times. Prayers and readings in this volume are numbered from 300 onwards.

Many people put to good use collections of prayers as well as anthologies of readings, but there are very few books – like this – of prayer services of themed prayers and readings. Draft copies of these prayer services have been very well-received, and I have been grateful for the constructive comments that people have offered. Amongst those who are likely to find the two volumes of help will be parish and retreat groups of all ages, catechists, teachers with older students, religious communities, and individuals in various circumstances.

Gathering in the Presence of God

The focus of these prayer services is such that each begins very clearly with the life-giving practice of reminding ourselves that we are in the Presence of God. We appreciate that it is not that we are *placing* ourselves in God's Presence; rather we are focussing on where we are already. God makes his home with us, abides with us, is to be found in our midst, is present when two or three gather in His name[1]. He promises to be with us always, for it is in him that we live and move and have our being[2].

Celtic and many other spiritualities focus on God's Presence, God-being-with-us in the ordinariness of daily life. The beautiful craftsmanship of Celtic manuscripts and crosses showing intertwining paths, draws us to focus on God's Presence being 'woven' throughout all the strands of our lives. Ongoing renewal of a sense of the Presence of God is essential for our walking with God: that warm relationship in which we are called *'friends of God'*[3] and *'see him face-to-face'*[4].

With the emphasis on initially reminding ourselves that God is with us, it is best that a hymn not precede the *Gathering in the Presence of God*, but be sung later at an appropriate time. At the back of the book (pg 142ff) some suitable hymns are listed for each prayer service, and I am reminded that one of the notes written by Johann Sebastian Bach (1685-1750) in the margins of his Bible, reads: *"Where there is devotional music, God with his grace is always present!"* And some will recall that Augustine commented that *"the one who sings well, prays twice!"*

The Need for Pauses

Words of the fourth verse (usually omitted from hymn books) of John Whittier's *Dear Lord and Father of mankind* remind us that other things – though often important – can obscure our need to pause and meet God in prayer:

> *"...All our words and works that drown*
> *The tender whisper of Thy call..."*

A choice has been made that each of the thirty two prayer services that form this book not be of too many words, lest the length promote a feeling of a need to 'get through' what is printed. Any such sense of haste would detract from one of the essential 'ingredients' of a prayer service, namely of having pauses, spaces: the better to slow down, reflect, sensitise ourselves and encourage us to 'allow' God opportunities to 'slip in'. *"The Divine Presence slips through the crevices between our words and judgements. Wall-to-wall spiritual talk leaves no oxygen for a living God to breathe"* (pg 274 of Eternal Echoes by John O'Donohue, Bantam Books).

Having avoided overcrowding of material also helps to convey that praying is not necessarily the same as saying prayers! We use words when helpful, but appreciate the need to allow God also to work through silence. All who are in love appreciate that much time is of silent pauses – not of nothingness, but of quiet time that reflects the warmth of a loving relationship in which words, though important, are not always necessary. Pausing also alerts us to have the attitude of listening, of being aware, of being open.

Selecting Materials

There is no need, of course, to use everything that is printed in a particular prayer service. The aim is to pray, and not necessarily to use all the words that are provided!

For convenience, sections of longer prayers have been numbered so as to be of help if taken in turn by two groupsor individuals. Numbering may also assist the sharing of lengthier readings. If readers know passages in advance, it is an encouragement for them to ponder and pray the reading before presenting it to the group. The numbering of items in the main text is discreet, reminding us that the book is designed to be very much more than an anthology of inspiring pieces: these are prayer services. Likewise, although authors are named beside texts, the precise source is listed at the back of the book (pg 146ff) so as to minimise distractions during the time of prayer.

Not all of the services include prayers of intercession. If it is decided to include a period of time for such spontaneous prayers, it is advisable before starting the prayer service to announce at what point that will be. Some people choose the Lord's Prayer to conclude a time of intercession. Good books of intercessions include David Adam's three volumes: *'Clouds and Glory'*, *'Traces of Glory'* and *'Glimpses of Glory'* (SPCK), and *'Prayers for All Seasons'* by Nick Fawcett (Kevin Mayhew).

Each service concludes specifically with a blessing, which may also serve to give a clear indication that the prayer service has come to an end. Most of these blessings are based on Scripture, from which much inspiration for the contents of this book has been derived.

An Appendix of this volume is entitled *The Final Journey*, and is a resource for inspiration and for accompanying the dying and those who mourn. Many have commented on how poignant is the use of *The Song of Farewell* (number 566).

A Way of Praying – especially with Scripture

Confronted these days with 'information overload', many of us feel the need for scanning and speed-reading as a means of detecting points in a text, or of judging which paragraphs should be read in full. There is a danger if we transfer this approach to the reading of the Scriptures. Far from seeking to glean *information*, we are aiming for *formation* of God's Word deep within. For too long there was a tendency to perceive the Scriptures simply as containing a moral or doctrinal message. Once such a 'message' had been 'picked up', some thought that the 'static' text had achieved its purpose. Yet *'the word of God is alive and active'*[5], as many come to know in their own lives.

As I pray in the simplicity of our own chapel, I find it very helpful that two spotlights have a particular focus: one on the Body of the Lord, reserved in one corner at the front, and another on the enthroned, open Word of the Lord in the other. Indeed, *'the Church has always venerated the Divine Scriptures just as it has venerated the Body of the Lord'*[6].

The process of repeating a passage slowly (preferably whispering it aloud, if alone, helping to sense both listening and proclamation), pondering it, and dwelling particularly on a couple of phrases, encourages us to allow the words to enter deep within us. There - and this is especially the case with Scripture – the Spirit can give flesh to that word and transform us to become more like the Father. This way of praying (a form of *Lectio Divina*, which can be explored readily on the Internet) is a means of 'allowing' God to touch our hearts and embrace us.

The key verb *to listen* (implying a knowing and realising deep within), occurs some 445 times through the Bible (JB). Conscious of the Lord's call for *"those who have ears to hear, to listen"*[7], we pray to be open to hear *'the still, small voice of God'*[8]. Our prayer is *"Speak, Lord, your servant is listening"*[9]. Having listened and heard and then *'pondered the words in our hearts'*[10], we pray for its fulfilment in our daily lives. *'As the rain and the snow come down from the heavens and do not return without watering the earth, so may God's word not return to him empty without carrying out his will, but succeed in what it was sent to do.'*[11] Lord, *"be it done to me according to your word."*[12]

A Conclusion

The world's largest Gothic arches in Liverpool's Anglican Cathedral help convey for me something of the magnificence of God. Yet their architect, Sir Giles Gilbert Scott, remarked: *"Do not look at my arches, but at the spaces they create."* It is hoped that this book may help us to dwell amongst the 'spaces' created, as well as in the words we use: giving an opportunity for the God of spaces to dwell fully in us and amongst us, filling whatever emptiness he finds there. May we be *'filled with the utter fullness of God'*.[13]

Brother Nicholas Hutchinson FSC
De La Salle House
83 Carr Lane East
Liverpool
L11 4SF
email: nicholas@prayingeachday.org
website: www.prayingeachday.org

1 – Jn 14[23], 15[3], 19[8], Mt 18[20]; **2** – Mt 28[20], Acts 17[28]; **3** – Wis 7[27], Jam 2[23];
4 – Gen 32[31], Ex 33[11], Num 14[14], Is 52[8], Rev 22[4]; **5** – Heb 4[12]; **6** – Vatican II: Dei Verbum, 21; **7** – Mt 11[15];
8 – 1 Kings 19[12]; **9** – 1 Sam 3[10]; **10** – cf. Lk 2[19];
11 – cf. Is 55[10-11]; **12** – Lk 1[38]; **13** – Eph 3[19]

Gathering in the Presence of God

NH 301

Let us pray:

God our Father,
    your promises of old
    gave your people hope
    that you would enter their lives anew.
We rejoice that Jesus, your Son,
    the fulfilment of your promises,
    can be found among us today.
We ask you to help us
    to open our hearts to him.

(pause)

Prayer – *The 'O' Antiphons*

Lucien Deiss 302

1 O Wisdom,
    issuing from the mouth of the Most High,
    announced by the prophets:
        Come to teach us the way of salvation.
        Come, O Lord: come, save your people.

2 O Lord,
    shepherd of the House of Israel,
    who guide your people:
        Come to redeem us by the strength of your arm.
        Come, O Lord: come, save your people.

3 O Son of David, standard of people and of kings,
    you whom the world implores:
        Come to deliver us, Lord; do not delay.
        Come, O Lord: come, save your people.

4 O Key of David, and Sceptre of the House of Israel,
    you who open so no-one can close,
    you who close so no-one can open:
        Come to free those who wait in darkness.
        Come, O Lord: come, save your people.

5   O Rising Sun,
    Splendour of Eternal Light, and Sun of Justice:
    Come to give light
    to those who are seated in the shadow of death.
    Come, O Lord: come, save your people.

6   O King of nations,
    Expectation of peoples, and Cornerstone of the Church:
    Come to deliver those whom you have created.
    Come, O Lord: come, save your people.

7   O Emmanuel,
    King and hope of nations, and Saviour of all people:
    Come to free us, Lord; do not delay.
    Come, O Lord: come, save your people.

303 Personal Reflection

Ann Wroe

1   The modern world has lost all patience with waiting. "Why wait?" cry the hoardings. "Don't hesitate. Have it now." We used to be content to wait a week to see our photographs, nine months to know the gender of our children... Now we no longer see any virtue in that sort of self-restraint. I often don't see any myself. I get furious behind slow drivers on the motorway, walk out of shops if there are not enough assistants... I still find no attraction in the word 'instant': like instant mashed potato, it's probably a sham, and I won't get into debt over any delusion of 'instant credit'...

2   At this time of year, the whole liturgy of the Church reflects the same dilemma. It is torn between desperately wanting Christ to come, and waiting in patience. *"The Spirit and the bride say, 'Come!'"*, reads one antiphon. Why wait? Yet the *'O' Antiphons* remind us that the waiting has gone on for centuries, and that the world and the elements have somehow adjusted to this routine of expectation. In its very slowness and sadness, the Advent Prose accepts the idea of delay. But (unlike waiting to be served, or for the bus) humankind waits in faith that the longed-for Saviour will and must appear in the end.

3   It also waits in a different mood. At Advent we are instructed to be awake and listen. This sounds like the antithesis of waiting, when we tend to switch off. But our waiting is meant to be active, highly sensitised to whatever may happen in apparently empty time. We are looking in the darkness for changes, signs of the new world to come, and we are listening in the silence for a voice.

Prayer

1   Every year, my God,
     your Church celebrates the holy season of Advent.
  Every year we pray those beautiful prayers
     of longing and waiting,
     and sing those lovely songs of hope and promise.

2   Every year we roll up
     our needs and yearnings and faithful expectations
     into one word: *"Come!"*

3   And yet, what a strange prayer this is!
  After all, you have already come
     and pitched your tent among us.
  You have already shared our life with its little joys,
     its long days of tedious routine, its bitter end.
  Could we invite you to anything more than this
     with our *"Come"*?

4   Could you approach any nearer than you did
     when you became the 'Son of Man',
     when you adopted our ordinary little ways so thoroughly
     that it's almost impossible to distinguish you
     from other human beings?

5   In spite of all this we pray: *"Come"*.
  And this word comes from the bottom of our hearts
     as it did long ago
     from the hearts of our forefathers,
     the kings and prophets
     who saw your day still far off in the distance,
     and fervently blessed its coming.

6   Indeed, your coming is promised
     in the very first pages of Holy Scripture,
     and yet, on the last page, there still stands the prayer:
     "Come, Lord Jesus".

Prayer

God, our loving Father,
     we thank you that your love for us
     is without limit or condition,
     and is greater than we could hope for or imagine.
You promised that light would shine in darkness.

Light in our hearts a flame of your love:
> love that will warm our families and homes,
> your love that will bring healing.
As we prepare in these days
> for the birth of Jesus, your Son and our Brother,
> we surrender to you the darkness in our lives.
Help us to turn our hearts to you
> and welcome Jesus into our lives anew. Amen.

306 Blessing

John Knox
(c. 1513-1572)

May the Lord sanctify us and bless us,
and may he pour the riches of his grace upon us,
that we may please him
and live in his love
to the end of our days. Amen.

The *'O' Antiphons* are sometimes sung during Advent, and they have become the *Alleluia verses* before the Gospel of the day for 17-23 December:

(O Sapientia)	O come, Wisdom of our God...
(O Adonai)	O come, Leader of Ancient Israel...
(O Radix Jesse)	O come, Flower of Jesse's Stem...
(O Clavis David)	O come, Key of David...
(O Oriens)	O come, Radiant Dawn...
(O Rex Gentium)	O come, King of all the Nations...
(O Emmanuel)	O come, Emmanuel...

Branches of a tree, ever-green
(using the Advent Wreath)

Gathering in the Presence of God

NH 307

Let us pray:

God our Father,
    we thank you for the promise made to your people
    to send us a Saviour.
Inspire us to prepare our hearts
    and wait in joyful hope
    for his coming anew into our lives.
Bless us as we gather in his name
    and consider the symbolism of this wreath,
    a sign of your promises
    that come to fulfilment in Jesus, your Son,
    the Light of our world. Amen.

(pause)

Prayer

David Adam 308

1   O Lord, give us yourself above all things.
    It is in your coming alone that we are enriched.
    It is in your coming that your true gifts come.
    Come, Lord, that we may share the gifts of your presence.

2   Come, Lord, with healing of the past,
    Come and heal our memories.
    Come with joy for the present,
    Come and give life to our existence.

3   Come with hope for the future,
    Come and give a sense of eternity.
    Come with strength for our wills,
    Come with power for our thoughts.

4   Come with love for our heart,
    Come and give affection to our being.
    Come, Lord, give yourself above all things
    and help us to give ourselves to you.

1 The death of an old year, the birth of a new,
   and ADVENT, the season of WAITING,
   waiting for God to fulfil his ancient promise
   to come and save us,
   and to complete the salvation already given us
   through Christ our Lord.

2 We wait impatiently through the winter months
   for the renewal of the earth,
   and for the birth of the Saviour in our hearts.

3 As a symbol of our waiting in hope
   we have made this wreath
   from the leaves of evergreen trees
   – leaves that remain green in winter
   and which the frost cannot kill.
   They are a sign of our new life in Christ
   and a reminder of his promise to be *ever* with us.

4 Our wreath is in the shape of a circle
   which, like the love of God, has no beginning or end.
   The wreath includes
   some leaves and berries and seeds
   of the old year that we have just completed,
   and which we now offer to God.

5 As we light the candles
   – one in each week of Advent –
   we remember the saints of the Old Testament
   who waited and waited in the darkness
   and did not give up their hope.
   And we remember those who suffer in darkness today:
   in the darkness of poverty or fear, of imprisonment or despair.

6 We shall see this wreath
   as a symbol of God's faithfulness
   in his promise to be ever with us,
   remembering that we are called to be the light of the world,
   and be a tree ever-green, with living branches joined to Christ,
   who is our light and our salvation:
   our King, crowned with a wreath of victory.

Intercessions

1   Loving Father, as we prepare in these days
for the coming of Jesus, your Son,
we surrender to you the darkness in our lives,
and wait in expectant hope:
>**Father, may your kingdom grow in our midst.**

2   You promised that light would shine in darkness.
Light in our hearts a flame of your love:
your love that will bring healing and life.
>**Father, may your kingdom grow in our midst.**

3   God of life, come to the wintery branches
where our lives bear no fruit,
where our efforts have failed,
where our courage has faltered,
where the sap of energy has died.
>**Father, may your kingdom grow in our midst.**

4   Father, we bring before you
those who wait and are disappointed;
those who experience a winter of despair;
those who are broken by sorrow and pain and suffering.
>**Father, may your kingdom grow in our midst.**

5   Father, we bring before you all who carry heavy burdens,
all whose mistakes dominate their lives,
all who are empty,
and all who wish to grow closer to you.
>**Father, may your kingdom grow in our midst.**

6   Show us, Father, how to level mountains
of superiority and domination,
and fill in the valleys
of those who sense little value and little hope.
>**Father, may your kingdom grow in our midst.**

7   As your Son will be revealed to the poor and simple,
help us, Father, to see your grandeur
in all your people
and in the ordinary events of life.
>**Father, may your kingdom grow in our midst.**

Our Father…

311 Blessing

Enlighten us now, God our Father,
 as we await the fulfilment of your promises
 in Jesus, your Son, your Word made flesh,
 the life and light of our world.
Bless us, Father,
 with the new life of Christ Jesus, our Savour,
 and give us your grace and peace. Amen.

Titus 14

Making the Advent Wreath:

Mention is made in Reading 309 that the Advent Wreath includes evergreen leaves and also some leaves, berries and seeds of the old year. The circular wreath holds four tall candles which are lit in turn as from each Sunday of Advent, until they are all alight. A fifth candle (often red) is at the centre, and is lit on Christmas Eve.

Nothing is impossible for God's love

Gathering in the Presence of God

Let us remember that we are in the Presence of God:
And let us adore him.

(pause)

Let us ask the Holy Spirit to pray in us:
Come, Holy Spirit; fill our hearts anew.

(pause)

Prayer

> Loving Lord,
> may I, like Mary,
> have the courage to face my unique blessedness.
> Teach me to listen and not to be afraid
> as you open me up
> to the wonder of my being,
> and bring Jesus to birth in my life.

Reading

1 How significant it would be for each of us to recognise the journey of Mary into our hearts so that we can sing and dance our own magnificats, the stories of the wonderful things God has done and revealed to our heart and invited us to become. Mary's magnificat is a model and pattern for all Christian prayer as it expresses her presence to herself, to God, and to all God's people. The magnificat tells of that three-fold journey of discovery and love. Mary comes to know and love herself. She is unafraid of speaking openly about this self – *"my soul... my spirit... he has looked upon me... all generations will call me blessed... the Almighty has done great things for me."*

2 Out of Mary's profound presence to *herself*, receiving the gift and sacrament of who she is, she is compelled to dance and sing her gratitude and celebration of what God has done, is doing, and will continue to do from age to age for ever.

3 Out of her presence to *God* she is present to the *anawim*, the powerless and the voiceless, the hungry and those in need of help. She dares to

prophesy that the proud of heart will be routed, the princes pulled down from their thrones, the rich sent empty away. God is faithful to his promises forever!

315 Prayer

Luke 14[6-55]

Terence Collins, FSC

Antiphon: Blessed are those who believe
that what the Lord promises them will be fulfilled.

I will praise the Lord because I am happy.
God is my Saviour, and he has honoured me.
From now on
everyone will say that I have been blessed.

God is so powerful
and he has done wonderful things for me.
Praise his holy name!

The Lord is always kind to us when we pray to him.
He helps those who are weak and hungry.
He humbles those who are proud of their riches.

He will always be merciful to us,
and he will protect those who serve him.

Glory be to the Father...

Antiphon: Blessed are those who believe
that what the Lord promises them will be fulfilled.

316 Reading

Bishop Pedro
Casaldaliga
source unknown

1 To say your name, Mary,
is to say that our needs captivate the loving attention of God.

2 To say your name, Mary,
is to say that the Promise has been raised on the milk of a woman.

3 To say your name, Mary,
is to say that our flesh clothes the silent presence of the Word.

4 To say your name, Mary,
is to say that the Kingdom is travelling hand in hand with History.

5 To say your name, Mary,
is to say that we're beside the Cross and ablaze with the Spirit.

6 To say your name, Mary,
 is to say that every name can be full of Grace.

7 To say your name, Mary,
 is to say that every death holds the promise of Resurrection.

8 To say your name, Mary,
 is to say that all is yours, Cause of our Joy!

Prayer

Peter de Rosa 317

1 Father,
 I thank you for what you have revealed of yourself
 in Mary's virgin-motherhood.

2 She was humble, so you exalted her;
 she was poor, so you enriched her;
 she was empty, so you filled her;
 she was your servant, so you cared for her.
 She had no future by reason of her virginity,
 so you brought to birth in her
 the world's future, Jesus Christ our Lord.

3 Mary responded to your message
 with faith and love.
 Behold, she said, the slave of the Lord.
 Let the Lord's Word be fulfilled in me.

4 Lord, through Mary's faith and love and humble service,
 your Word was made flesh
 and dwelt among us.

5 You exalted Mary your slave
 who humbled herself in her virginity,
 as you were to exalt your slave Jesus
 when he humbled himself
 even to the death of the cross.

6 Father, I pray that through the Virgin Mary
 I may learn what you expect of me.
 May I become, through grace,
 humble and poor,
 empty and a slave,
 so that you may exalt and enrich me,
 so that you may fill me with heavenly blessings

and bring Christ to birth through faith
in my heart.

318 Prayer

Lucien Deiss

We bless you, God our Father,
for having loved the Virgin Mary so much.
Through her
we too find favour with you
in her son, Jesus,
who became our brother.
Send down upon us your Holy Spirit
so that we, too,
might become the temple of your glory
and that Jesus might be born in our hearts through faith.
For nothing is impossible for your love.

319 Blessing

NH

May God
from whom all blessings flow
send us his Word each day of our lives.
May that Word grow to fulfilment
by the power of the Holy Spirit,
and may God bless us,
take away our fear,
and lead us to grow in faith and love. Amen.

"I must decrease and he must increase"
– *John the Baptist points the way forward*

Gathering in the Presence of God

Let us pray:

> Here in your presence, Lord,
>   we can live more fully
>   as we 'decrease' in significance
>   and let you 'increase'.
> Lead us now
>   to grow more aware
>   that you choose to be with us.

(pause)

Reading

> This is what Isaiah says:
> *'A voice cries out:*
> *"In the wilderness prepare a way for the Lord.*
> *Level the mountains and fill in the valleys.*
> *Make the uneven ground level*
>   *and so make a straight road in the desert*
>   *for our God to approach*
>   *and come amongst us.*
> *From the top of a high mountain*
>   *proclaim that God is approaching:*
>   *yes, he is coming amongst us.*
> *This is his promise, and he is faithful to what he says."'*

Prayer

1 Loving Father,
       by the power of your Spirit
       bring down our false pride
       and level any mountains of superiority in our lives.

2 Lift us up, great God,
       from valleys of regret and despair.
   Raise us from our sinfulness
       and from the holes into which we fall.
   Raise us from all that blights us

and makes us less than fully human
according to the image of Jesus, your Son.

3   Restore our balance, Lord,
        and release us from anything
        that overwhelms or diminishes us.
    Lead us to prepare a straight path
        for the coming anew into our lives
        of Jesus, your Son. Amen.

323 Personal Reflection

Mary's cousin, Elizabeth, gives birth to a son whom she and her husband,
Zechariah, agree to name 'John'. The *'Benedictus'* is the name given to the
words spoken by Zechariah to his week-old son, who will become known as
John the Baptist. Zechariah is filled with the Holy Spirit as he prophesies and
blesses his own son whom he addresses as *"you, little child"*. We can think
of those on whom we would like to pray a blessing.

324 The Benedictus – *The Song of Zechariah*

Luke 16$^{7-79}$
GNB

1   Let us praise the Lord, the God of Israel!
    He has come to the help of his people
    and has set them free.

2   He has provided for us a mighty Saviour,
    a descendant of his servant David.
    He promised through his holy prophets long ago
    that he would save us from our enemies,
    from the power of all those who hate us.
    He said he would show mercy to our ancestors
    and remember his sacred covenant.

3   With a solemn oath to our ancestor Abraham
    he promised to rescue us from our enemies
    and allow us to serve him without fear,
    so that we might be holy and righteous before him
    all the days of our life.

4   You, my child,
    will be called a prophet of the Most High God.
    You will go ahead of the Lord
    to prepare his road for him,

5   To tell his people that they will be saved
    by having their sins forgiven.
    Our God is merciful and tender.

Gathering in the Presence of God

NH
cf Rev 21

329

Let us pray:

ALL   We rejoice, Lord,
            that you have chosen
            to make your home among us
            and call us your people.
        In the vision of a new heaven and a new earth
            there is no temple in the city
            because you, Lord God, are the city's temple.
        And your city has no need
            for the sun or moon to shine on it,
            for your glory is its light.
        The nations will walk by its light,
            and the kings of the earth
            will bring their glory into it.
        We rejoice, Lord,
            that you have made your home among us
            and are with us now.

(pause)

Reading

Dietrich Bonhoeffer   330

From the Christian point of view there is no special problem about Christmas in a prison cell. For many people in this building it will probably be a more sincere and genuine occasion than in places where nothing but the name is kept. That misery, suffering, pove , loneliness, helplessness, and guilt mean something quite different in t   es of God from what they mean in our judgement, that God will ar   where people turn away, that Christ was born in a stable because   s no room for him in the inn – these are things that a prisoner c   tand better than other people. For him they really are glad tidin   t faith gives him a part in the communion of saints, a Christian   p breaking the bounds of time and space, and reducing the m   nfinement here to insignificance.

Meditatic

Isaiah 9[1-7a]   331
NRSV

    1   ple who walked in darkness
            een a great light;
            e who lived in a land of deep darkness
            on them light has shone.

2   You have multiplied the nation,
     you have increased its joy;
     they rejoice before you
     as with joy at the harvest,
     as people exult when dividing plunder.

3   For the yoke of their burden,
     and the bar across their shoulders,
     the rod of their oppressor,
     you have broken as on the day of Midian...

4   For a child has been born for us, a son given to us;
     authority rests upon his shoulders.

5   And he is named
     Wonderful Counsellor, Mighty God,
     Everlasting Father, Prince of Peace.
     His authority shall grow continually,
     and there shall be endless peace.

332 Reading

Henri Nouwen

I keep thinking about the Christmas scene that has been arranged under the altar. This is probably the most meaningful crib that I have seen. The woodcarved figures are made in India: a poor woman, a poor man and a small child between them. The carving is simple, nearly primitive. No eyes, no ears, no mouths, just the contours of the faces. The figurines are smaller than a human hand – nearly too small to attract attention at all. But then a beam of light shines on the figures and projects large shadows on the walls of the sanctuary. That says it all. The light thrown on the smallness of Mary, Joseph and the Child projects them as large hopeful shadows against the walls of our life and our world. Without the radiant beam of light shining into the darkness, there is little to be seen. We might just pass by these simple people and continue to walk in darkness. But everything changes with the light.

333 Prayer

Ray Simpson

(taken in turn;
all joining in each concluding sentence)

1   Child of Glory, Child of Mary,
     born in the stable, King of all;
     you came to our wasteland, in our place suffered.
     We greet you our Saviour, Brother and Lord.

2 Your birth binds heaven and earth together;
   bind us together in the kinship of one family
   throughout the world.
   > **May we be one with creation
   > and one with all peoples.**

3 Your birth made possible the Holy Family.
   > **Make families whole and holy today.**

4 Babe of Heaven, defenceless Love:
   You had to travel far from home.
   > **Strengthen us
   > as we make our pilgrimage of trust on earth.**

5 King of glory, you accepted such humbling.
   > **Give us a serving spirit in all we do.**

6 Your birth shows us
   the simplicity of the Father's love,
   the wonder of being human.
   > **Help us to live fully human lives for you.**

Personal Reflection

about Cardinal Basil Hume **334**

At the annual celebration of carols in Westminster Cathedral, Cardinal Hume climbed into the pulpit to preach. Moved by the beauty of the candlelight and the singing of the choir, the congregation awaited a homily about the Christmas story. Instead, the cardinal spoke about a concentration camp. He described a small gypsy girl, clutching a doll, waiting in line for the gas chambers. He told how a guard, watching the little girl cry, found his heart changed. The guard stripped off his clothes and walked into the gas chamber to die with the girl, holding her hand. "Together", the cardinal said, "they triumphed over death and over evil and found the paradox of death leading to life."

Intercessions

NH   **335**

1 Let us pray for those who are crippled by shame or guilt,
   for those imprisoned by their mistakes,
   and for those haunted by the past
   or oppressed by sadness.
   Let us pray for the sick, the impoverished,
   the bereaved and those approaching death.
   > **Turn the darkness into light before us, Lord,
   > and rocky tracks into paths that are smooth.**

Is 42[16]

2 Let us pray for those who call evil 'good'
and good 'evil',
who substitute darkness for light: Is 5²⁰
that love and light may change their lives.
Let us pray for ourselves,
that the Lord may bring his light
into whatever dark areas are concealed in our lives.
Turn the darkness into light before us, Lord,
and rocky tracks into paths that are smooth.

3 Let us pray for all God's people,
that it may be with kindness and tenderness
that we look at ourselves.
And let us pray for our world which God loves so much, Jn 3¹⁶
that the light of Christ
may shine like a city on a hilltop. Mt 5¹⁴
Turn the darkness into light before us, Lord,
and rocky tracks into paths that are smooth.

336 Blessing

NH

May God the Father of all light
and Jesus, the Light whom the darkness cannot overcome,
and the Spirit who enlightens all people,
bless, guide and protect us this day
and throughout our lives. Amen.

The Word was made flesh

Gathering in the Presence of God

Henri Nouwen   337

Through the Incarnation of God in Jesus Christ all human flesh has been lifted up into God's own intimacy. There is no human being in the past, present or future, in East, West, North or South, who has not been embraced by God in and through the flesh of the Word.

> *Let us pause to reflect that the God of love embraces us warmly*
> *as the individuals we are.*

(pause)

Prayer

Michael Hollings   338

Wisdom 18[14]

Almighty God, Father of Light,
    your eternal Word leapt down from heaven,
    blazing out the generosity of your love
    in the deep silence of the night.
We, your Church, are filled with wonder
    at your nearness to us,
    our nearness to you.
Open our hearts to receive his life
    and increase our vision with the rising dawn.
In this way
    may our lives be filled
    with the glory and peace of Jesus Christ. Amen.

Personal Reflection

Oscar Romero   339

The 'flesh' is the concrete person. The flesh is we who are present here – people just beginning to live, the vigorous adolescent, the old man nearing the end. The flesh is marked by time. The flesh is the actual human situation, human beings in sin, human beings in painful situations, the people of a nation that seems to have got into a blind alley. The flesh is all of us who live incarnate.

And this flesh, this frail flesh that has beginning and end, that sickens and dies, that becomes miserable or happy – that is what the Word of God became. The Word was made flesh.

340 Prayer

Kathy Galloway

1 Lord Jesus, it's good to know
that you lived in the flesh,
walked where we walked, felt what we feel,
got tired, had sore and dirty feet,
needed to eat
and think about where the next meal was coming from.

2 But it's even better to know
that you enjoyed your food,
the feel of perfume on your skin,
the wind on your face,
a child in your arms,
and good wine at a wedding.

3 You didn't mind when people touched you,
even those who were thought of as unclean,
and you kissed people with diseases.

4 Thank you for understanding our bodily pains and pleasures
and for valuing them.

341 Meditation

John Powell

(taking a paragraph in turn)

1 I want to tell you about the Word of Life.
I want to tell you what I have heard with my own ears,
and what I have seen with my own eyes.
Yes, I have seen the Word
and my hands have actually touched him.   1 Jn 1[1]
I have seen his always-faithful goodness
through the works of love which he performed.   Jn 5[19-20]

2 Jesus kept insisting with us
that his Kingdom was a matter of faith.   Jn 6[29]
He invited us to see everything through the eyes of faith.
And he asked us to risk our lives
on the only real force in this world,
the force of love.   Jn 13[34-35]

3 He assured us that he is the way, the truth, and the life,   Jn 14[6]
and that if we followed him
we would never walk in darkness.

Jesus is the truth, the perfect revelation of the Father,
 and he shares with us
 the very life of God that is in him.   Jn 1^{17},14^{6},17^{6}

4 Slowly we came to know a God of love
  because Jesus introduced us
  to the meaning and the reality of love,
  and we gradually learned to accept
  a whole new way of looking at things,
  a whole new vision of reality.

5 We Christians are those who know this truth
  because we see through the eyes of faith,
  and we have put on the mind of Jesus.   1 Jn 2$^{3-6}$

6 It is this truth, this vision, that sets us free
  – free from all crippling prejudices
  that wither the human spirit…
 The truth of Jesus sets us free
  from the tyranny of possession
  by the things of this world.
 His truth enables us
  to rise above the weakness of our human nature. Jn 8$^{31-34}$, 1 Jn 2^{4}

7 This is the truth that sets us free
  and gives our lives meaning,
  the truth that makes sense of this world
  and puts a song in our hearts:

ALL *We ourselves know and believe*
   the love which God has for us.
  God is love, and whoever lives in love
   lives in union with God,
   and God lives in union with him…
  There is no fear in love;
   perfect love drives out all fear.   1 Jn 4$^{16,\,18}$; GNB

Personal Reflection   Karl Rahner **342**

 God has entrusted his last, deepest,
 and most beautiful word to the world,
 in the Word made flesh.
 This Word says: I love you world, man and woman.
 I am there. I am with you.
 I am your life. I am your time.

I weep your tears. I am your joy.
Do not be afraid.
When you do not know how to go any further,
I am with you.
I am in your anguish, because I suffered it myself.
I am in your need and your death,
because today I began to live and to die with you.
I am your life.
I promise you: for you, too, life is waiting.
For you, too, the gates will open.

343 Blessing   NH

We thank you, Father,
   for the touch of your hand
   on the clay of the earth
   that formed our bodies,
   and for the breath of your Spirit
   giving life to our flesh.
We thank you for restoring our dignity
   in Jesus, your Son, your Word made flesh,
   whose image you see whenever you look at us.
Bless us now, Father, Son and Holy Spirit. Amen.

The poverty of shepherds and the abundance of God

Gathering in the Presence of God

NH   344

Let us pray:

> In the fullness of time, Father,
>> you sent Jesus, your Son,
>> to dwell amongst us, flesh of our flesh.
> Lead us to grow more attuned
>> to his presence with us
>> now and every day.

(pause)

Personal Reflection

Oscar Romero   345

No-one can celebrate a genuine Christmas without being truly poor. The self-sufficient, the proud, those who – because they have everything – look down on others, those who have no need even of God: for them there will be no Christmas. Only the poor, the hungry, those who need someone to come on their behalf, will have that someone. That someone is God, Emmanuel, God-with-us. Without poverty of spirit, there can be no abundance of God.

Prayer

A prayer from Uganda   346
source unknown

> Blessed are you, O Christ Child,
> that your cradle was so low
> that shepherds,
> the poorest and simplest of people,
> could yet kneel beside you
> and look, level-eyed, into the face of God.

Reading

Mark Link, SJ   347

THE CRIB OF FRANCIS OF ASSISI

> 1   In a cave on a windswept Italian mountainside,
>> Francis of Assisi assembled the first Christmas Crib in 1223.
> The Christ-Child, placed on an altar of stone,
>> and two live animals – an ox and a donkey –
>> were its only occupants.
> Today, a tiny friary surrounds the cave
>> which still remains relatively undisturbed by the years.

2 The idea behind the crib
   was to make the story of Jesus' birth more vivid
   in the minds of the shepherds and farmers who lived there.
The people were enthusiastic.
They were the ones who suggested the ox and donkey.
Thomas of Celano, one of Francis' companions,
   wrote about the opening of the crib:

3 "The friars from different localities had come.
The men and women of the place
   brought candles and torches to illuminate the night.
Lastly the saint arrived, saw the preparations,
   and was happy.
The crib was put in place, the hay brought in,
   and the ox and donkey were led forward.
Simplicity was honoured, poverty exalted, humility praised…

4 The woods rang with voices
   and the rocks echoed the hymns of joy.
The saint, vested as the deacon of the Mass,
   chanted the Gospel.
He preached to the people
   about the poor King of Bethlehem.
At the end of the vigil,
   everyone returned to their homes full of joy."

348 Prayer
Denis Blackledge, SJ

(read in turn)

1 *'Do not be afraid.*
Listen, I bring you news of great joy,
   a joy to be shared by the whole people.
Today a Saviour has been born to you;
   he is Christ the Lord.
And here is a sign for you: you will find a baby
   wrapped in swaddling clothes and lying in a manger.'

2 Loving Lord,
   what a God of surprises you are!
Let me stop for a few moments and ponder this story.
Let me jump into the frame and become a shepherd.
No wonder they were terrified out of their wits:
   why should God be interested in them,
   such ordinary and sinful and messy human beings?
No wonder they needed to be told: *'Do not be afraid.'*

3 Perhaps that's part of my problem, Lord.
  Do I really believe that you love me as I am,
    warts and all?
  You don't wait until I'm perfect (whatever that might mean)
    before you say you love me, Lord.
  Help me to believe that staggeringly simple
    and simply staggering fact.

4 Come to think of it, my whole life and purpose is built
    on the *'news of great joy"*
    (a *'joy to be shared by the whole people'*)
    that I'm hearing just now as a shepherd…

5 *'Listen'* was the first thing they were asked to do, Lord.
  You asked them to stop, to ponder, to marvel
    at what was happening all around them.
  You asked them
    to open the eyes of their minds and hearts
    so as to hear in the depths of themselves
    and make living sense of this *'news of great joy'*.

6 And the news was not for tomorrow's world
    – it was precisely for *'Today'* –
    here, now, for me and for all the people:
    news to be spread and shared and enjoyed.
  So I'm listening, Lord. What do I have to do now?

7 The answer is so simple that I can miss it.
  'Here is a sign for you: you will find a baby...'
  In finding Jesus, my Saviour, our Saviour,
    precisely as a baby,
  I am healed of so much that is nonsense in my life.

8 In bringing myself before this infant
    who is so vulnerable and so dependent,
    so human and so innocent,
    I am faced with the challenge of really listening
    to the impact this Christ-Child
    is just now having on my life.

ALL   Give me the courage this Christmas, Lord,
**   to get on the knees of my mind and heart**
**   and begin to put you at the centre of my life. Amen.**

349 **Prayer**

Donal Neary, SJ

I pray, Lord, that the simplicity of your presence
   will bring to birth in me and in others
   a compassion for the poor,
   a hunger for justice among the oppressed,
   and a real desire for brotherhood among nations.
May this Christmas be a time
   of sincere reconciliation,
   of lasting forgiveness,
   of deep-rooted joy.
May it be the smile of God,
   and the fragrance of your holy presence among us all.

350 **Blessing**

cf Phil 1[2]

May God our Father and the Lord Jesus Christ
   give us grace and peace
   this day and always. Amen.

May Christ be born in me today

Gathering in the Presence of God

Denis Blackledge, SJ   **351**

Let us pray:

>Loving Lord,
>>your touch and your hold
>>are closer than a human embrace,
>>closer than a kiss,
>>closer than a heartbeat,
>>closer than a breath.
>Loving Lord,
>>let me let myself be held by you.

(pause)

Meditation

David Konstant   **352**

1   Every birth is truly a miracle.
Each birth marks God's entry into the world.
A new-born child is made in the image of God, is made for God,
and is only fully alive when knowing God as Father in heaven.

2   This birth is the perfect sign that God is with us.
God has spoken.
His Word has been given to the world.
This is a mystery to ponder, a wonder to marvel at,
a glory to sing about.
"Glory to God in the highest, and peace to his people on earth."

3   It scarcely seems credible that this child,
born in such simplicity,
recognised by only a handful of shepherds,
should be Saviour... Son of God... God-with-us...
the Image of the invisible God,
the last revelation of God to mankind.
But so he is.

4   I need to understand that God reveals himself to the poor and simple,
that it is the ordinary things of life
– a smile, a word; forgiveness, freedom;
life itself and the whole of creation –

which show the grandeur of God,
that it is because he was born in poverty and simplicity
that I have the courage to approach him,
for he is like me in all things except sin…

5 What my friends are looking for is often so simple,
so ordinary, and so human,
that I have not grasped that their search is truly for God,
the Word made flesh.

6 Let me try to become a better witness to God's presence,
to see him in the world he has made,
to meet him in others,
to know him through his eternal Word,
and so to proclaim him by my daily living.

ALL *May Christ be born in me today.*

353 **Personal Reflection**

Geoffrey Preston, OP

Jesus… is the face of God.
In him,
immensity was cloistered in the dear womb of Mary,
and at last we knew
what it was to be a human being.

354 **Prayer**

Greek Orthodox prayer

Lord our God,
the angels bring their song,
the heavens bring their star,
the shepherds bring their wonder,
the animals give their manger,
the wise men bring their gifts,
and we human beings bring the Virgin-Mother.
We bring our whole selves to you
who have so fully and generously
given yourself to us. Amen.

355 **Reading**

Edward Farrell

1 Incarnation is open to us; Christ is alive in his body – the Church. Christ comes alive in us as we become free enough to give him our heart… Every time we act in such a way as to reveal God, every time we abandon ourselves into God's hands, we participate in Incarnation. Each time we celebrate the liturgy, the Sacraments of the Church, we live the mystery of the Incarnation…

2   Living through the commemoration of Jesus' life, we are born into the mystery of his life in us. How do you give birth to Christ? How do you act as midwife to his birth in others? Do you nurture him as the child within you, care for him as the child in others? Do you allow him to discipline you, to help you to grow? How do you assist or abet his growth in your family, your friends, your enemies?

3   Have you spent lonely days in the desert with him, struggling to resist temptation? Are you an angel feeding him in your neighbour? Have you allowed Satan to speak through you to separate another from him?

4   How do you carry his cross? Are you free enough to be vulnerable to another helping you shoulder your cross? Who have you nailed to the cross? Can you sit with the women at the cross, and wait with the women at the tomb, and wait for the Resurrection?

5   Are you at home when the Spirit breathes a word in you? Who will you follow? Are you free to plunge into the Incarnation? How do you live the mysteries of Incarnation from Christmas to Easter, from Easter to Pentecost?

Prayer

Catherine Moran, HFB   356

1   God our Father,
> in the Holy Family of Nazareth
> you embraced our world with great tenderness and love,
> and renewed family life
> in the pure and noble dignity
> you intended from the beginning.

2   To Mary and Joseph
> who walked the path of faith
> with courage and fidelity,
> you entrusted Jesus, your Son,
> who would grow in stature and wisdom
> and in favour with all.
Enfolded in the love and warmth of that family
> the beginnings of our redemption took hold.

3   Lead us to grow
> in the warmth and gentleness of the Holy Family,
> that 'gentle image of the Trinity',
> poor in the eyes of the world,
> rich in the treasures of heaven,
> hidden and unknown on the earth,
> contemplated by the angels.

4   Like Jesus, Mary and Joseph
        who contemplated your will, Father, as it unfolded,
        may we, too, hold your Word,
        ponder it in our hearts,
        and respond with courage and generosity
        as Jesus makes his home in us.

5   Deepen our love for one another
        and enable us to live in peace, Father,
        united with you and with each other.

ALL   *Inspired by the way of life of Jesus, Mary and Joseph,*
              lead us to treasure what is most deeply human.
          Teach us the sanctity of human love
              and show us the value of family life
              that we may share in your love and life forever. Amen.

357 **Blessing**

This day
may we live so close to Jesus
that those who touch our lives
may touch him.
And may the God of love and peace   2 Cor 13[11]
be with us all,
now and always. Amen.

The end of an old year;
the start of a new

Gathering in the Presence of God

NH 358
cf Rev 21

Let us pray:

> We come before you, Lord Jesus,
>> knowing that you are already here
>> because you have chosen to dwell among us.
> You are the Alpha and the Omega,
>> the Beginning and the End,
>> and you renew all things.
> Lead us to encounter you anew
>> as we come to the end of an old year
>> and the start of a new.

(pause)

Prayer

Frank Topping 359

1 The old year is dying;
>> even now the troubles of last year
>> are fading into the past to be forgotten.
> Yet there is much to be remembered with gratitude.

2 In this coming year
>> I'd like to be able to sort out my life,
>> to throw away yesterday's mistakes
>> and keep the good things…

3 I can't count the things I was going to do
>> or stop doing, or give up.
> But I'm reluctant to give up anything.
> I cling to the things I want,
>> forgetting that fragile gifts
>> held in a possessive grip usually break.

4 Lord, help me not to cling so fiercely
>> to the things I claim as mine,
>> when even the breath I breathe is yours.
> Lord of all time,
>> help me to give back the life I owe to you…

5   Give me courage to offer this year
        and everything in it, to you
        – the things I may enjoy,
        and the things I may suffer.

ALL   ***Let me, from this day,***
        put my whole life into your hands –
        triumphs and failures,
        laughter and tears:
        they are all at your disposal.
    From this time
        let me be no longer my own,
        but yours.

360 Prayer

Francis Brienen

1   God of all time,
        who makes all things new,
        we bring before you the year now ending.
    For life full and good,
        for opportunities recognised and taken,
        for love known and shared,
        we thank you.

2   Where we have fallen short, forgive us.
    When we worry over what is past, free us.

3   As we begin again
        and take our first few steps into the future,
        where nothing is safe and certain except you,
        we ask for the courage of the wise men
        who simply went and followed a star.
    We ask for their wisdom
        in choosing to pursue the deepest truth,
        not knowing where they would be led.

4   In the year to come, God of all time,
        be our help and company.
    Hold our hands as we journey onwards
        and may your dream of Shalom
        – where all will be at peace –
        be our guiding star. Amen.

Reading

Minnie Louise Haskins **361**

I said to the man who stood at the gate of the Year:
    "Give me a light
    that I may tread safely into the unknown."
And he replied:
    "Go out into the darkness
    and put your hand into the hand of God.
That shall be to you
    better than light,
    and safer than a known way."
May that almighty hand
    guide and uphold us all.

Prayer

Denis Blackledge, SJ **362**

1   Loving Lord,
    whatever else you are,
    you are a God who is on the move.
There are so many signs of life,
    movement, freshness, newness.
What a wonderful gift it is
    to belong to a pilgrim people
    led by a Pilgrim God!...

2   You give us the power
    to feel our way to you
    because you are always coming
    to meet and greet each one of us.

3   Loving Lord,
    as we look back on this past year
    and look forward to a new year,
    we can rest and remember gratefully
    and notice all those ways
    in which you have moved us along,
    closer to you and to one another,
    sometimes in spite of ourselves.
And we can look forward eagerly
    to your moving us on a little more...

4   Loving Lord,
    keep us always aware
    that you are with us
    every step of our pilgrim way.
Keep us all moving closer
    to you and to one another. Amen.

363 Blessing

attributed to
Cardinal John Henry
Newman

May he support us all the year long,
   till the shades lengthen
   and the evening comes
   and the busy world is hushed
   and the fever of life is over
   and our work is done.
Then, in his mercy,
   may he give us a safe lodging
   and a holy rest
   and peace at the last.

Another suitable prayer is that by Leslie Brandt (number 209 in Volume 1), changing
'day' to 'year' in three places.

Epiphany

– visitation, manifestation, showing forth, unveiling, revelation

Gathering in the Presence of God

NH   364

Let us pray:

> Lord, you have led us here
> > to this time and place
> > to honour you in prayer.
> Lead us now on that greater journey
> > which is to our hearts,
> > that we may discover there
> > the riches of your presence.

(pause)

Reading

John O'Donohue   365

The Shawshank Redemption is a film about friendship in a depressing prison setting. Every kind of brutality operates there. In that prison the sounds are sinister and the silence is eerie. One day a prisoner who is working in the library manages to get into the main office. He locks the door and puts on a piece of wonderful classical music, a duet from Mozart's *Marriage of Figaro*, and plays it over the loudspeaker into the prison yard. As if from the eternal spheres, like an invisible manna, this beautiful music falls onto all the haunted lives in this dreary place. All the prisoners stop, entranced, and listen. There is pure silence and stillness to receive the full visitation of the music. This is a moment of pure *epiphany*. The visit of the music is such a surprise. In the lovely shock of its beauty, the lost grandeur of creation is suddenly present. This is a moment of pure wonder in a dark world.

Prayer

Denis Blackledge, SJ   366

1   Loving Lord,
> help us to be wise individuals,
> people who can show to others
> the difference that your coming to us as a baby makes.

2   Help us to show the extraordinary in the ordinary.
> Help us to be openers of our treasures,
> > just as the wise men were openers of theirs.

3   Especially, Lord,
> help us to open more richly and deeply

the treasure that is our own selfhood,
and help us all to see the extraordinary rich depths
that each person is
in the ordinariness of everyday living.

ALL   *Help us to become*
       better dreamers and better delighters
       in the treasures you present to us each day. Amen.

367 Personal Reflection

NH

The Apollo 11 astronauts were the first to walk on the moon. When the three returned to Earth in 1969, many nations wanted to welcome them. Neil Armstrong, 'Buzz' Aldrin and Michael Collins made a tour of many countries.

Pope Paul VI presented the three astronauts with porcelain statues of the Three Wise Men of the Epiphany. Buzz Aldrin later said that this was one of the most moving moments of their 23-nation tour, as Pope Paul compared them with the Three Wise Men who had followed the star to find Jesus in Bethlehem, remarking that the three astronauts had reached their destination by navigating according to the distant stars.

368 Prayer

Lucien Deiss

*(to be read in turn, with all joining in
the last line of each verse)*

1   Today the Wise men come to Bethlehem.
     With them, Lord,
     we come to render homage to you.
        Glory and praise to you, Lord Jesus Christ!

2   Today the star leads them to the manger.
     With them, Lord,
     we wish to let ourselves be led by your light.
        Glory and praise to you, Lord Jesus Christ!

3   Today they see the little Child and Mary, his mother.
     With them, Lord,
     we wish to discover you in the midst of our brothers and sisters.
        Glory and praise to you, Lord Jesus Christ!

4   Today they prostrate themselves before you, and adore you.
     With them, Lord,
     we wish to adore your holy will for us.
        Glory and praise to you, Lord Jesus Christ!

5 Today they offer him their gifts.
  With them, Lord,
  we wish to offer you our own lives as a gift.
  Glory and praise to you, Lord Jesus Christ!

Personal Reflection

W. H. Auden 369

To discover how to be human now
Is the reason we follow this star.

Intercessions

David Adam 370

1 Great and wonderful God, we seek you.
  We look for you. We long for you.
  We come and offer our lives, our love, our hopes to you.
  God, richer than all we have to offer, we offer you our worship.
  We give thanks for the offering of *frankincense*
      and pray for all who give their lives in adoration.
  We pray for the congregation and church to which we belong.
  We pray for all leaders of worship,
      for all who bow in quiet adoration.

  **By the light of your presence,
  fill us with your glory.**

2 O God, Creator of all things, we offer you all we have received.
  We offer our talents, our possessions, ourselves in your service.
  We give you thanks for the gift of *gold*.
  We pray for all who work in commerce…
      and we remember before you the world's poor,
      the bankrupt, the underprivileged, the starving.
  May all who have received of your bounty
      share generously with those in need.

  **By the light of your presence,
  fill us with your glory.**

3 O God, you share in our sorrows,
      you enter into our darkness.
  You, Lord, come to redeem, release and restore us.
  We give thanks for the strange gift of *myrrh*.
  We pray for all who are in pain or in distress,
      all who are troubled or anxious.
  We pray for all who seek to relieve pain,
      for doctors, nurses and dentists.
  We pray for all who work for the redeeming of our world.

By the light of your presence,
fill us with your glory.

4 O God, whose Son was born into an earthly family,
    bless our homes and our loved ones.
  Reveal your presence in our homes and in our relationships.
  We pray for all who are born into sordid homes
    or into homelessness.
  We pray for children who suffer from violence or through neglect.

By the light of your presence,
fill us with your glory.

371 **Blessing**   NH
  God our Father,
    the star of Bethlehem
    was a sign of faith for the Wise Men.
  May we, too, perceive the vision you lay before us,
    knowing that Jesus himself is the Way,
    and enable us to remain committed on the journey to its end.
  And so we ask for
    the richness of your blessing, Father,
    that we may grow in faith and wisdom
    and discover Jesus in our midst each day. Amen.

In turn, the Three Wise Men could be placed with the other crib figures at the start
of the first three paragraphs of number 370, the intercessions by David Adam.

Gathering in the Presence of God

NH   372

Let us pray:

> We read in the Gospel, Lord,
>> that you went away to lonely places to pray.
>
> In my busy days of noise and action
>> and with burdens upon my shoulders,
>> remind me of my need for time alone,
>> for peace and quiet within,
>> for time to be alone with you.
>
> Remind me that you are with me now.

(pause)

Prayer

Peter de Rosa   373

(each taking a paragraph)

> 1   Father, when I look back on my life
>> I see in how many ways I have offended you
>> and failed to love.

> 2   I am thankful
>> that you never deal with us according to our sins.
>
> As high as the heavens are above the earth,
>> such is the height of your unchanging love
>> towards those who respect you.

> 3   As far as the east is from the west,
>> so far do you remove from us our sins.
>
> For you are our gentle and forbearing Father,
>> and as a Father pities his children,
>> so do you, Lord, pity us…

> 4   I ask you to create in me a clean heart
>> and put a new spirit within me.
>
> Do not cast me away from your presence
>> nor take your Holy Spirit from me.

> 5   It is true, Father, I have often sinned,
>> but I pray for a sincere and heart-felt sorrow.

The sacrifice acceptable to you is a broken spirit;
    a broken and contrite heart you will not spurn.

6 Father, you are the high and lofty One
    who inhabits eternity, whose name is holy.
But Christ came from on high
    to call sinners like me,
    and he who is our Friend assures us
    that you will live in everyone
    who tries to do good to others
    and who has a contrite spirit and a humble heart.

374 Personal Reflection

Evelyn Underhill
source unknown

Penetrate these murky corners
    where we hide our memories and tendencies
    on which we do not care to look,
    but which we will not yield freely up to you,
    that you may purify them and transmute them:
    – the persistent grudge,
    – the half-acknowledged enmity which is still smouldering,
    – the bitterness of that loss we have not turned into sacrifice,
    – the private comfort we cling to,
    – the secret fear of failure which saps our initiative
       and is really inverted pride,
    – the pessimism which is an insult to your joy.
Lord, we bring all these to you,
    and we review them with shame and penitence
    in your steadfast light.

375 Prayer

Frank Topping

1 *'Out of the depths I call to you,*
    Lord, hear my cry for help.
Listen compassionately to my pleading.
If you never overlooked our sins,
    who could survive?
Lord, help me to start again.

Ps 129 (130)

2 Your forgiveness wipes my slate clean.
Your love blots out all my sins
    as if they had never happened.

3 Your forgiveness is like re-birth,
    a chance to start again with a new, fresh life.
I have only to ask

and your forgiveness is immediate.
Lord, teach me to forgive as I am forgiven…

4   Teach me your life-giving generosity.
No matter who is right or who is wrong,
    help me to sweep away the bitterness,
    the nurtured anger,
    the stored-up resentment of years.
Enable me to start again.

5   *'Out of the depths I call to you,*
    Lord, hear my cry for help.
Listen compassionately to my pleading.
If you never overlooked our sins,
    who could survive?'

6   Lord, help me to forgive and be forgiven.
Help me to start again.

Reading

Anthony Padovano   376

Prayer reaches our lives as we begin to do the things we could not have done unless we had prayed. We begin to believe, we seek forgiveness, we love those who would otherwise have been unlovable to us, we attend to the important things in life. Prayer is not a pious addition to things we would have done anyway. It is a force allowing things to happen which could not have occurred without it.

Personal Reflection

anonymous – found   377
beside a dead body in
Ravensbruck
concentration camp

O Lord,
    remember not only the men and women of good-will,
    but also those of ill-will.
But do not remember all the suffering they have inflicted on us
    – remember the fruits we have bought thanks to this suffering:
    our comradeship, our loyalty,
    our humility, our courage,
    our generosity,
    the greatness of heart which has grown out of all this.
And when they come to judgement,
    let all the fruits that we have borne
    be their forgiveness.

378 Prayer

NH

God our Father,
I know that to forgive someone
can be far from being an easy option,
and I know that forgiveness
isn't somehow pretending
that something wrong hasn't happened.
For what I have done wrong, Father,
forgive me in the same way
that I am generous and gracious in forgiving
– or truly hoping to forgive –
those who have done wrong to me.
Empower me to break the cycle
of any hatred, resentment or bitterness,
always resisting evil
and conquering it with goodness. Amen.

379 Blessing

cf Eph 6[10]

May the Lord bless us
and enable us to grow strong in him. Amen.

Some might like to place on a table a dish of ashes (perhaps best moistened into a paste). At an appropriate time during the prayer service, each person could use the ashes to trace the cross on their forehead.

Alternatively a bowl of water could be used and, with a towel available, each could dip their hands into the water as a sign of God's cleansing and our repentance.

Gathering in the Presence of God

Fr Flann Lynch OFM Cap **380**

(Prayer of Abundance)

Let us pray:

Father, Son and Holy Spirit,
I adore you, I love you.
I thank you for the wonder of my being
and for the miracle of your presence in me.

(pause)

Prayer

Frank Topping   **381**

1 Lord, you have said:
*"Come to me all you who are heavily laden
and I will give you rest."*

2 This day in your presence, Lord,
I lay the burden of my doubts,
all unanswered questions,
all the problems of my conscience,
the wrongs that I have done to others,

3 the guilt of things neglected,
the pain of cruel words,
the stupidity of my pride and vanity,
the arrogance and conceit of my selfishness,
my little faith, my lack of love.

4 Lord, I am not worthy to be in your presence;
say but the word and I shall be healed.

5 Lord, this day in your presence
I look for forgiveness, I look for help.
Help me to love;
help me to serve;
help me in my suffering;
help me to trust.

ALL   **May your forgiving love
live in me,
that it might no longer be I that live
but you who live in me.**

382 Reading

Anthony Bloom

At rock-bottom we are made in the image of God, and this stripping is very much like the cleaning of an ancient, beautiful wall painting, or of a painting by a great master that was painted over in the course of the centuries by tasteless people, who had intruded upon the real beauty that had been created by the master. To begin with, the more we clean, the more things disappear, and it seems to us that we have created a mess where there was at least a certain amount of beauty; perhaps not much, but some beauty. And then we begin to discover the real beauty which the great master has put into his painting. We see the misery, then the mess in between, but at the same time we have a preview of the authentic beauty. And we discover that what we are is a poor person who needs God; but not God to fill the gap – God to be met.

383 Prayer

Lucien Deiss

(each to take a paragraph; all joining in the response)

1   You come to look for the lost sheep;
    joyfully you carry it on your shoulders.
    We beg you:
        O God, be merciful to me, a sinner!

2   You go to meet the prodigal son;
    you clasp him in your arms and kiss him.
    We beg you:
        O God, be merciful to me, a sinner!

3   You choose as your apostle, Matthew the tax-collector.
    You have not come to call the righteous, but sinners.
    We beg you:
        O God, be merciful to me, a sinner!

4   You enter the house of Zacchaeus, the tax-collector,
    in order to seek out and save what was lost.
    We beg you:
        O God, be merciful to me, a sinner!

5   You accept the ointment of the sinful woman.
    Because of her tears you pardon and defend her.
    We beg you:
        O God, be merciful to me, a sinner!

6   To the good thief who implores you,
    you open the gate of Paradise –
    We beg you:
        O God, be merciful to me, a sinner!

Personal Reflection

Michael Mayne **384**

Sin is our refusal to become who we truly are. In those moments when I kneel before God in penitence, or join with others in confession, sometimes I am aware of specific faults: unloving words, thoughtless conduct, selfish actions. I am aware of not caring enough. But chiefly I am aware of a much more subtle temptation: to settle for less than I might be. To choose the lesser good. To lack curiosity and wonder. To miss the mark because my sights are fixed too low. Not to perceive that I am 'fearfully and wonderfully made' in God's image. And when I ask God to forgive me, I do so because, in settling for less than I am created to be, I know not what I do.

Prayer

NH   **385**

1 Loving Father,
you tell us in the Bible
that whatever wrongs we have done
you tread down our faults
and cast our sins to the bottom of the sea.

Mic 7[19]

2 We know there is no need
to keep thinking
about what we have done in the past,

Is 43[18]

because you pardon
the wrongs we have done,
and you delight in showing mercy.

Mic 7[18]

3 Lord, you love
all that you have made,

Wis 11[24]

and it is your very nature
to love and forgive.
You bind up all our wounds

Ps 147[3]

and you renew us by your love.

Zeph 3[17]

4 Lead each of us every day
to look upon ourselves and one another
in the same gracious way
that you smile and look upon us.

5 Remind us each day, Father,
that nothing can ever separate us from your love

Rom 8[31-39]

as we see it in Jesus, your Son. Amen.

386 Prayer

Mark Link, SJ

Merciful God,
like the prodigal son
I come home in sorrow.
I have sinned
against you and your people.

With the help of your grace,
I promise to try
to walk in the light of your presence,
and avoid whatever might lead me back
into darkness. Amen.

387 Blessing

NH

Forgiving Father,
Redeeming Son,
Sanctifying Spirit,
bless and guide and protect us
this day and always. Amen.

Transfiguration

(e.g. for the Second Sunday of Lent,
whose Gospel is the Transfiguration)

Gathering in the Presence of God

In May 1953 the top of Mount Everest was reached for the first time. The climbers were Tenzing Norkay, a Nepalese guide, and Edmund Hillary, a New Zealander. Later in life Tenzing Norkay said:

> *"It is with God himself*
> *as it is with a great mountain.*
> *The important thing*
> *is to come to him not with fear,*
> *but with love."*

Let us rest in God's love as we gather in his Presence.

(pause)

Prayer

Peter de Rosa

1 Jesus took Peter, James and John with him;
    and there, on a rocky height,
     he was transfigured.
  No launderer ever made clothes so white.

2 And there appeared in Jesus' glow
    Elijah, most renowned of prophets,
    and Moses who gave Israel her law.

3 Peter, foolish and unthinking, said:
    "Master, we are glad we came.
    We'll make three arbours here, one for each of you."

4 From the cloud above them, Father, your voice came:
    "This is my beloved Son; listen to him."
  And when the disciples looked,
    they saw no-one but Jesus.

5 Father, I thank you for this gospel story
    which illustrates so well Christ's sovereignty.
  I believe, Lord, that in everything he says and does

he lights up and fulfils the law and the prophets;
and it is enough now to listen to him.

6 For Jesus is your Christ,
even though death and dereliction
are waiting for him in Jerusalem.
It will be dark there,
and on another hill, shaped like a skull,
two other men will be beside him.

7 From his unclothed body no light will radiate;
and even you, Father, will be silent,
except for the one Word you will be saying to us
in the tremendous love of Jesus crucified.

390 Personal Reflection

Nelson Mandela

We are born to make manifest the glory of God that is within us. It's not just in some of us; it is in everyone. And when we let our own light shine, we subconsciously give other people permission to do the same.

391 Prayer

Denis Blackledge, SJ
reflecting on
Andrew the Apostle
Luke 9$^{28-36}$

1 Loving Lord,
I was one of the twelve specially chosen by you.
And, along with John and Peter,
there were intimate moments you chose to share
just with the three of us.
We saw your glory at the Transfiguration.
We saw your agony in the Garden of Gethsemane.
Those two key moments are seared in my memory.
The three of us almost missed everything:
both times we were almost asleep!

2 Both occasions stand out, Lord,
because you took us with you
when you went to pray.
You let us into the secret
of your relationship with the Father,
with the God you called 'Abba'.

3 You showed us Moses and Elijah,
the two great men of the Old Testament
who led and prophesied.
You let us hear their story
of how you would achieve your glory.

4   It was too awesome for words,
        and I remember my annoyance with Peter
        when he couldn't keep his mouth shut
        and just enjoy the privilege of being there.
    Then all was dark, cloudy, terrifying.
    And from that darkness came words:
        'This is my Son, the Chosen One.
        Listen to him.'
    And when we dared to look up,
        there you were, Jesus, on your own.

5   Loving Lord,
        that time with you on the mountain-top
        taught me how to listen.
    It gave me a fresh understanding
        of my own privileged relationship with you.
    I felt so much on the inside.
    I began to look on you as a pilgrim,
        as vulnerable, as human, as favoured Son.

6   That moment kept me going
        when I wanted to give up.
    It prepared me for Gethsemane.
    It enabled me to face forgiveness.
    It helped me to face you as the risen Lord.

7   Loving Lord,
        your Transfiguration taught me
        that my relationship with the Father echoes yours.
    By my heartfelt listening
        I learned the meaning of my own chosenness.
    I began to see that my prayer
        is nothing other
        than myself in my relationship with you,
        becoming a good listener, learner and responder
        to such an extent that others see *'only Jesus'*.

Blessing   John O'Donohue   **392**

1   May we be blessed in the holy names
    of those who carry our pain up the mountain of transfiguration.

2   May we know tender shelter and healing blessing
    when we are called to stand in the place of pain.
    May the places of darkness within us be surprised by light.

3   May we be granted the wisdom to avoid false resistance,
    and when suffering knocks on the door of our life
    may we be able to glimpse its hidden gift.
    May we be able to see the fruits of suffering.

4   May memory bless and shelter us
    with the hard-earned light of past travail,
    and may this give us confidence and trust.

5   May a window of light always surprise us.
    May the grace of transfiguration heal our wounds.

6   May we know that even though the storm might rage
    not a hair of our head will be harmed. Amen.

Being transformed in Christ

(e.g. for Holy Thursday and for the feast of The Body and Blood of Christ)

B14

Gathering in the Presence of God

NH 393
cf Jer 14[9]

Let us pray:

> Lord, you are in our midst
>> and we are called by your name.
> Touch our minds and hearts
>> and ask your Holy Spirit to pray in us.

(pause)

Personal Reflection

Sister Briege McKenna 394

1 The important aspect of the Eucharist is not what I do, but what Jesus does, and what I allow him to do in me. I must let the loving Jesus heal me and transform me through his body and blood. It is not my effort alone, but his action, that transforms me.

2 I realised this truth while attending an outdoor Mass in a mountainous Latin American country. Many very poor people came to this Mass. The priest was using an old table for an altar. A little boy was brought there who was suffering from very severe burns and sores on his body. I remember thinking, *"There's really nothing that can be done. It's so bad. We have no doctors or medicine here…"*

3 We prayed with the little boy, then the priest said to the old woman who had carried him to the Mass, *"Just leave him under the table here, and let's continue with the celebration of the Eucharist."* As we approached the Consecration, I had my eyes closed. When I opened them, I discovered that people were prostrate on the ground. They lifted up their eyes to adore the Lord. The look on their faces made me think, *"They really believe that this is Jesus."*

Prayer

C. I. Pettitt 395

1 Lord, we bring our work to your working hands.
We bring our sickness to your healing hands.

2 We bring our weakness to your strong hands.
We bring our sadness to your tender hands.

3 We bring our needs to your praying hands.
   We bring our suffering to your wounded hands.

4 We bring our love, our families and our children
   to your hands – outstretched to bless.

5 We bring our hands to share with you
   that Bread of Life which we take from you,
   that we may take your sacramental presence
   to share with others.

6 As we take your hands,
   we are to be those hands in the world today.

396 Reading *(continued)*

Sister Briege McKenna

1 After the Mass I went around to see how the little boy was. He had been placed under the table which served as the altar... I looked at the child, and he was fine. There wasn't a thing wrong with his little body. I said aloud, but more to myself, *"What happened to him?"* The old woman looked at me and said, *"What do you mean, 'What happened?' Didn't Jesus come?"*

2 During this Mass, as in all Masses, the priest had put his hands over the bread and wine, and he called upon the action of the Spirit to make this action holy *"that it may become the body and blood"* of Jesus. When the priest said this prayer, the Holy Spirit came, but he of course was not limited to do only what the priest asked. The Spirit also put his power over the little boy, and the boy was changed. He was healed and made whole.

3 That same day, at the beginning of Mass, I also saw a little boy who had a terrible facial deformity. At the end of Mass, his mother came running up to me with her child in her arms. She said, *"Sister, look at my little boy."* The boy's face was healed... Like the woman in the gospel, they came to Jesus with an expectant faith.

397 Prayer

Charles de Foucauld
(1858-1916)

Father, I abandon myself into your hands;
   do with me what you will.
Whatever you may do, I thank you:
   I am ready for all, I accept all.
Let only your will be done in me
   and in all your creatures –
   I wish no more than this, O Lord.
Into your hands I commend my soul;

I offer it to you with all the love of my heart,
for I love you, Lord, and so need to give myself,
to surrender myself into your hands without reserve,
and with boundless confidence,
for you are my Father.

Personal Reflection

Edward Farrell   398

If only the bread and wine is changed and nothing happens in us, is that not
a contradiction of the Eucharist?

Prayer

NH   399

God our Father,
  transform our poverty in the wealth of your love,
  our sinfulness in the healing of Jesus,
  and our weakness in the power of your Spirit.
Create new miracles this day
  as we place ourselves into your all-powerful hands.
Transform our lives
  that we may become the people you call us to be. Amen.

Personal Reflection

abridged from   400
Dom Gregory Dix

1 People have found no better thing to do than this
    for kings at their crowning
    and for criminals going to the scaffold;
    for armies in triumph
    and for a bride and bridegroom in a little country church;

2 for the wisdom of the parliament of a mighty nation,
    and for a sick old woman afraid to die;
    for a student sitting an examination
    and for Columbus setting out to discover America;

3 while the lions roared in the nearby amphitheatre
        before martyrdom;
    and while the hiss of scythes in the thick June grass
    came faintly through the windows of the church;

4 for the soul of a dead lover
    and in thankfulness because a relative did not die of pneumonia;
    by an exiled bishop who had hewn timber all day in a prison camp,
    and on the beach at Dunkirk in 1940.

5 And, week by week,
    on a hundred thousand successive Sundays,

priest and people gather together,
faithfully and unfailingly,
to carry out this command:
"Do this in memory of me."

401 Blessing

NH

Loving Lord,
beside you at the table of your Last Supper,
we are joined
by generations of your faithful people down the ages,
and by many brothers and sisters
across the world this day
who have been able to follow your command
to celebrate the Eucharist in memory of you.
We join you
in giving thanks to our Father
for so much in our lives.
We give thanks for your broken body which makes us whole,
and for your blood poured out which gives us life.
Bless us this day, Lord, and always. Amen.

The darkness of Gethsemane

Gathering in the Presence of God
Hugh Kay   **402**

The darkness you are encountering is in itself a rich experience. If it be that you really want to meet our Lord, then it is by moonlight that you must seek Him under an olive tree. You will find Him flat on the ground, and you will have to lie down on your face with Him if you are to catch His words.

Let us remind ourselves that he is with us now.

(pause)

Prayer
Denis Blackledge, SJ   **403**

Loving Lord,
    you fell flat on your face in a garden.
You know agony from the inside out.
Let me remember that there's nowhere
    where you haven't already been
    when it comes to being fully human.
At such moments, Lord,
    let me not be too proud
    to fall flat on my face beside you
    and let your agony begin to soak up mine.

Personal Reflection
Cardinal Basil Hume   **404**

If you have never been through darkness, then you simply cannot speak to people about the light. If you have never been through doubt, you probably cannot speak eloquently about faith. You have to know that side of life – the crucifixion side, the passion side – in order to speak eloquently about the resurrection side.

Prayer
NH   **405**

God our Father,
    we pray for those in great difficulty at this time.
It is out of the depths
    that some cry out to you in their desperation,
    and others find themselves unable to pray.
Lead them – lead all of us – Lord,
    to experience the depth of your love and affection.
Lift us up, Lord God,
    as you would lift Jesus from death
    to the new life of the Resurrection.

406 Prayer

Reinhold Neibuhr

God, grant me the serenity
to accept the things I cannot change,
courage to change the things I can,
and the wisdom to know the difference;

living one day at a time,
enjoying one moment at a time,
accepting hardship as the pathway to peace,
taking as He did, this sinful world as it is,
and not as I would have it;

trusting that He will make all things right
if I surrender to his will;
that I may be reasonably happy in this life,
and supremely happy with Him forever in the next.
Amen.

407 Personal Reflection

Sister Helen Prejean, CSJ
with a prisoner about
to be executed

The old Priest says prayers in Latin and takes a Communion wafer from the container and places it on Pat's tongue, then another into my outstretched hands. *"The Body of Christ,"* he says. *"Amen."* Yes, in this place I believe you are here, O Christ, you who sweated blood and who prayed aloud and in silent tears for your Father to remove your own suffering. This man about to die is not innocent, but he is human, and that is enough to draw you here.

408 Prayer

Peter de Rosa

1 Father, when Jesus sensed his hour was at hand,
   he went with his disciples to Mount Olivet.
   "You will all fall away," he said,
   but Peter proclaimed: *"The rest may fall away, but I will not."*

2 And Jesus replied: *"Peter, this very night before cock-crow,
   three times you will deny me."*
   "No, Lord," cried Peter. *"I would die with you,
   but I will not deny you."*

3 Then he who had lifted his head, and boasted like a cock,
   nodded and slept three times in Gethsemane.
   When Judas came with an armed guard to arrest his Master,
   Peter, with all the rest, ran off into the night.

4 Soon afterwards, in the courtyard,
   Peter denied his Master three times
   at the taunt of a serving maid.

5   While he was still uttering his oath, the cock began to crow.
And the Lord turned to Peter, and Peter remembered his words:
"Before cock-crow, three times you will deny me."
And he went out and wept bitterly.

6   Father, give me the light and strength of your Spirit
to resist temptation,
to repent like Peter immediately I fall,
and to know that Christ whom I repeatedly deny
is always looking at me
ready to forgive me unto seventy times seven.

Reading

John O'Donohue   **409**

Through choice Jesus gathered into the circle of his heart the pain of the world. This is horribly evident in his inner torture and fear in Gethsemane. Something awful happened in that garden. He sweated blood there. He was overcome with doubt. Everything was taken from him. Here the anguished scream of human desolation reached out for Divine consolation. And from the severe silence of the heavens, no sheltering echo returned. This is what the Cross is: that bleak, empty place where no certainty can ever settle. His friends betrayed and abandoned him. Christ explores the endless heart of loss with such gentle and vulnerable courage.

Prayer

St Richard of Chichester   **410**

Thanks be to you, my Lord Jesus Christ,
for all the benefits which you have given me,
for all the pains and insults
which you have borne for me.
O most merciful Redeemer, Friend and Brother,
may I know you more clearly,
love you more dearly,
and follow you more nearly,
day by day.

Blessing

NH   **411**

May the Lord Jesus Christ,
abandoned, denied and betrayed by his friends,
now bless us
and, with his Spirit,
empower us to live the qualities of his Kingdom. Amen.

Also appropriate is an excerpt from 'An Autobiography' by Agatha Christie (William Collins, 1977; page 150) , which is quoted on page 10 of the Introduction to 'Praying Each Day of the Year' by the present author and publisher.

The way that leads to the Cross

Gathering in the Presence of God

NH 412

Let us pray:

Lord, you call us by name
 and beckon us to follow you
 – not to walk alone,
 but to walk with you.
Touch our hearts and minds
 so that we may appreciate
 that you choose to walk beside us
 in the ordinary ways of our daily lives.
Thank you for being with us now.

(pause)

Prayer *(each taking a paragraph)*

Evelyn Underhill 413
1875-1941
source unknown

1 The pinnacle of the Temple is a very lonely place.
 You will not be waiting for me there.

2 Your method, your prayer,
  your disclosure of God,
  take the lowliest path.
 Your tabernacle among us
  is in the cave and the cottage.

3 I must come down like Zacchaeus
  if I would have you dwell with me,
  on the country roads of Galilee,
  in the villages and on the shore.
 Down among the cares, the sins,
  the labours and sufferings of ordinary people
  – there we shall find you.

4 *'O teach me your ways*
  and hold up my going in your paths
  that my footsteps slip not.'

5 Your paths are well-trodden.
 Along them you and your saints
  have carried healing and love
  to ordinary men and women where they are.

6 Teach me to serve them as you serve –
    with patience and simplicity,
    with reverence and love.

7 Your saints never presumed
    to grasp at their spiritual privileges,
    or use them for their own advantage,
    nor sought extraordinary grace.
  They loved to follow you along ordinary ways.
  Help me to love those ways, too.

8 Your Spirit is not given
    that we may escape life's friction and demands,
    but so that we may live the common life
    as you would have it lived
    – on earth as it is in heaven.

414 Reading

'Rule for a New Brother'

You are called to follow Jesus closely. With him you will take the road up to Jerusalem, the city of suffering and glorification. With him you will give everything that the Kingdom may come. On this road, you are called to be least of all and not master, to carry other people's burdens and not lay your own on them, to give freedom instead of taking it, to grow poor in order to make others rich, to take the cross upon yourself – thus bringing joy to others, to die in order that others may live.

415 Personal Reflection

John 14[6]

With 300,000 young people, Pope John Paul II attended a special rock concert in Italy in the late 1990s. Bob Dylan, famous for his song *'Blowin' in the wind'* was one of the performers, and the Pope referred to the song's opening words, saying:

    " *'How many roads must a man walk down?'*
    I answer: 'One!'
    There is only one road for us,
    and it is the road of Jesus Christ, who said:
    'I am the Way, the Truth and the Life.' "

416 Prayer

Erasmus

Lord Jesus Christ,
  you have said
  that you are the Way, the Truth and the Life.
Do not allow us to stray from you, who are the Way,
  nor to distrust you, who are the Truth,
  nor to rest in anything other than you,
  who are the Life.

Meditation – 'A narrow way'

1 The path of discipleship is narrow,
  and it is fatally easy to miss one's way and stray from the path,
  even after years of discipleship.
  And it is hard to find.
  On either side of the narrow path, deep chasms yawn.
  To be called to a life of extraordinary quality, to live up to it,
  and yet to be unconscious of it, is indeed a narrow way.

2 To confess and testify to the truth as it is in Jesus,
  and at the same time to love the enemies of that truth
  – his enemies and ours –
  and to love them with the infinite love of Jesus Christ,
  is indeed a narrow way.

3 To believe the promise of Jesus
  that his followers shall possess the earth,
  and at the same time to face our enemies,
  unarmed and defenceless,
  preferring to incur injustice rather than do wrong ourselves,
  is indeed a narrow way.

4 To see the weakness and wrong in others,
  and at the same time refrain from judging them;
  to deliver the gospel message without casting pearls before swine,
  is indeed a narrow way.

5 The way is unutterably hard,
  and at every moment we are in danger of straying from it.
  If we regard this way
  as one we follow in obedience to an external command,
  if we are afraid of ourselves all the time,
  it is indeed an impossible way.

6 But if we behold Jesus Christ going on before, step by step,
  if we only look to him and follow him, step by step,
  we shall not go astray.

7 But if we worry about the dangers that beset us,
  if we gaze at the road, instead of at him who goes before,
  we are already straying from the path.
  For he is himself the way, the narrow way and the strait gate.
  He, and he alone, is our journey's end.

8　When we know that,
　　we are able to proceed along the narrow way
　　through the strait gate of the cross,
　　and on to eternal life,
　　and the very narrowness of the road
　　will increase our certainty.

418 Blessing

NH

1　Along the ordinary paths of my life, Lord,
　　　you accompany me,
　　　sharing my joys and my sorrows,
　　　my hopes and my fears.

2　It is to you
　　　who have already been before me
　　　that I turn:
　　　you who say
　　　that the burden for those who follow you
　　　is light.

3　In your strength, Lord,
　　　and with you at my side,
　　　I shall walk where you wish me to walk.
　　And when I fall,
　　　I know that it will be you
　　　who will bend low and reassure me
　　　and lift my cross onto your shoulders.

4　Empower me with your Spirit and bless me,
　　　and re-awaken in me each day
　　　the joy and enthusiasm that arise
　　　from knowing deep in my heart
　　　that you are my Way, my Truth and my Life.

5　Renew in me each day, too,
　　　the sense of being thankful always
　　　for the many blessings in my life. Amen.

"Only a suffering God can help"

B17

Dietrich Bonhoeffer

Gathering in the Presence of God

419

In Luke's Gospel, in shared suffering, the Good Thief on the Cross is the only person who addresses Jesus by his name rather than by a title of respect. Suffering is a great 'leveller', and sufferers in common are brothers and sisters.

Let us pray:

NH

> Like the Good Thief
> I, too, am beside you, Jesus,
> simply as I am.
> Take my prayer to your heart as I say:
> "Jesus, remember me
> when you come into your kingdom."

Lk 23⁴²

(pause)

Reading

Donal Neary, SJ   420

The cross is the sign that all Christians recognise. It's a reminder of God's love breaking through the violence of the world. It's a sign that no greater love can exist than to suffer with others. It's the sign of the completeness of God's care, for it went beyond death. It's a symbol of hope and of courage – the one thing to which we can all raise our eyes and be consoled, comforted and challenged. It has done this for centuries because of the Man who made it famous. This Sign of the Cross is how we welcome our children into life, and send our dying people forward to eternity. It's a sign of hope, not of death; the man on it is a king. Rather than a picture of degradation, it is a throne. We allow ourselves to look at this sign, to be touched by it. Let it move us to be loving, to burn for justice, to forgive us our sins. It is the great sign of reconciliation, people touching God from earth to heaven, people reaching out to each other, from one corner of the world to another.

Prayer

Peter de Rosa   421

1 Father, in sympathising with Christ on his cross
>   we are sympathising with suffering people everywhere.

2 We are joining our prayers to the prayers of
>   the hungry and the thirsty,
>   the hurt and the lonely,
>   the sick and the dying,
>   the outcasts and the refugees.

3   We are uniting ourselves
        with all who are oppressed,
        all the known innocents who are condemned to death,
        all who are betrayed by their friends.

4   We are sharing in the pain
        of all who are adjudged fools
        by the people they have served all their lives,
        all who are nailed to the cross
        of others' sins and stupidities,
        all who feel in their hearts
        that you, God, have abandoned them.

5   We believe that Jesus Christ, your Son,
        is also the Son of Man.
    We believe that, in him,
        all mankind has suffered, been humiliated, and died.
    But we are confident, too,
        that by his bruises all of us are healed.

6   That is why, Father, we take our place
        at the foot of his cross,
        knowing that Good Friday is really good
        because of him who loved us
        and gave himself up for us.

422 Personal Reflection

If Jesus Christ is not true God,
how could he help us?
If he is not true man,
how could he help us?

Dietrich Bonhoeffer
1906-1945

423 Prayer

NH

*(We can pray alongside Job of the Old Testament
and beside Jesus on the cross,
and for people who are suffering today)*

1   Father,
        my faith isn't strong enough to move mountains
        but I join my little faith
        to that of countless others.
    I pray from the confidence
        of knowing deep in my heart
        that *'you endowed me with life,
        and watch each breath of mine
        with tender care.'*

Mt 21[21]

Job 10[12]

2   Today I place myself
          beside all those who need strength and healing:
          those who are sick,
          those who are tortured and in pain,

living water of the Spirit

a psalm:

ry terrible crosses,
ken.

ering in the Presence of God
pray:

Holy Spirit,
who hovered over the waters of the earth,
ready to turn chaos into beauty,
lead us in our prayer
and stir us up at this time
to appreciate that you are in our midst,
you in whom we live and move and have our being.
Amen.

ent:

s been dear to them.

t be day?"
wly evening comes!"   Job 7[4]

          those who have *'fear come over them,*
          at the thought of all they suffer.'   Job 9[28]
   I pray for all who have *'terrors turn to meet them,'*
          whose *'confidence is blown away as if by the wind,'*
          whose *'life trickles away,*
          as they are gripped by days of grief.'   Job 30[15-18]

6   Words are not easy, Father,
          when difficulties overwhelm your people.
   In place of my words,
          take the deepest longings of my heart,
          and hear the words instead of Jesus, your Son,
          your Word made flesh,
          who calls us his friends,   Jn 15[14]
          and wishes his peace and joy upon us.   Jn 14[27], 17[13]

ALL   Father, this prayer is made
          for our brothers and sisters in torment,
          knowing that Jesus, our Brother,
          said that you love us   Jn 17[23]
          as you love him. Amen.

WALK IN MY PRESENCE   67

424 Prayer

Sheila Cassidy

Lord of the Universe, Master of All,
    look in love upon your people.
Pour the healing oil of your compassion
    on a world that is wounded and dying.
Send us out in search of the lost,
    to comfort the afflicted,
    to bind up the broken,
    and to free those trapped
    under the rubble of their fallen dreams.

425 Blessing

cf 2 John 1[3]

May God the Father
and Jesus Christ, the Father's Son,
give us grace, mercy and peace
now and always. Amen.

By his wounds we are healed

Isaiah 53[5]

Gathering in the Presence of God

Let us pray:

> Lord Jesus,
> > in coming among us
> > you did not seek to explain suffering
> > but you filled it with your presence
> > and changed people's lives.
> Lead us to grow more aware of your presence
> > in all that is ordinary
> > – today and each day of our lives.

(pause)

Reading and Prayer

David Konstant

1 It is said that the condemned prisoner carried only the cross-piece,
> which was lashed to his arms...
> The vertical post stayed in position at the top of the hill.

2 The horizontal – a reminder
> that, like Christ, I am on a pilgrim journey...
> that, like Christ, I cannot always choose the way...
> that, like Christ, I carry with me a burden I cannot lose...

3 The vertical – a reminder
> that God is always there...
> that all I do in the end is to give him glory...
> that my journey to heaven must be rooted in the ground...

ALL **Lord, see that I 'do not follow the wrong path,
and lead me in the path of life eternal'.**

Prayer

Lucien Deiss

(each taking a paragraph, and all joining in the response)

1 Lord Jesus, in agony in the Garden of Olives,
> troubled by sadness and fear,
> comforted by an angel:
> > **Have mercy, Lord, have mercy on us.**

2 Lord Jesus, betrayed by Judas' kiss,
  abandoned by your apostles,
  delivered into the hands of sinners.
    Have mercy, Lord, have mercy on us.

3 Lord Jesus, accused by false witnesses,
  condemned to die on the cross,
  struck by servants, covered with spittle:
    Have mercy, Lord, have mercy on us.

4 Lord Jesus, disowned by Peter, your apostle,
  delivered to Pilate and Herod,
  counted among the likes of Barabbas:
    Have mercy, Lord, have mercy on us.

5 Lord Jesus, carrying your cross to Calvary,
  consoled by the daughters of Jerusalem,
  helped by Simon of Cyrene:
    Have mercy, Lord, have mercy on us.

6 Lord Jesus, stripped of your clothes,
  given vinegar to drink,
  crucified with thieves:
    Have mercy, Lord, have mercy on us.

7 Lord Jesus, insulted on the cross,
  praying for your executioners,
  pardoning the good thief:
    Have mercy, Lord, have mercy on us.

8 Lord Jesus, entrusting your mother to your beloved disciple,
  giving up your spirit into the hands of your Father,
  dying for all of us sinners:
    Have mercy, Lord, have mercy on us.
    By your sufferings, Lord,
    heal the wounds in our hearts.
    Let your tears be a source of joy for us,
    and let your death give us life.

429 Personal Reflection

Elie Wiesel

1 The SS seemed more preoccupied, more disturbed than usual. To hang a
  young boy in front of thousands of spectators was no light matter. The
  head of the camp read the verdict. All eyes were on the child. He was
  lividly pale, almost calm, biting his lips. The gallows threw its shadow

over him... The three victims mounted together on the chairs. The three necks were placed at the same moment within the nooses. *"Long live liberty!"* cried the two adults. But the child was silent.

2 *"Where is God? Where is he?"* someone behind me asked. At a sign from the head of the camp, the three chairs tipped over; total silence throughout the camp. On the horizon the sun was setting. *"Bare your heads!"* yelled the head of the camp. His voice was raucous. We were weeping. *"Cover your heads!"* Then the march past began. The two adults were no longer alive. Their tongues hung swollen, blue-tinged. But the third rope was still moving; being so light, the child was still alive...

3 For more than half an hour he stayed there, struggling between life and death, dying in slow agony under our eyes. And we had to look at him full in the face. He was still alive when I passed in front of him. His tongue was still red, his eyes not yet glazed. Behind me I heard the same man asking, *"Where is God now?"* And I heard a voice within me answer him: *"Where is he? Here he is – he is hanging here on these gallows..."*

Prayer

Frank Topping   **430**

1 It is easy to believe that God is for us on a sunny day,
   on a holiday when family and friends surround us.
   But alone, with winter's rain on the windows,
   when nothing is going right,
   then it is hard to accept the idea that *'God is for us'*.
   Yet it was in the bleakness of a crucifixion
   that God revealed the love that remains constant,
   even in the darkest hour.

2 Men and women have faced persecution and imprisonment;
   have resisted the torments of wickedness,
   strengthened only by faith
   in the promise that God is with us to the end of time.
   Illness and calamity of every description have been endured
   in the knowledge that *'God is for us'*.

3 If the gates of hell cannot prevail against his word,
   then no trial that I face,
   no pain, no problem, can ever defeat the love of God.

4 Lord, in the difficulties that surround me,
   in the decisions I have to face,
   in the struggle to survive in what sometimes seems a hostile world,
   may I have faith enough to declare with confidence:

ALL *'If God is for us, who is against us?*
For I am convinced that neither death, nor life,
nor angels, nor principalities,
nor things present, nor things to come,
nor height, nor depth;
no, nothing in all creation
can separate us from the love of God in Christ Jesus our Lord.'

Rom 8

431 Blessing

cf 1 Thess 5^{23-28}

May the God who gives us peace
    make us holy in every way
    because he is faithful.
And may the grace of our Lord Jesus Christ
    be with us always. Amen.

Gathering in the Presence of God

432

Let us remind ourselves that Jesus approaches us with open arms, and is with us now.

(pause)

Reading and Prayer

David Konstant   433

Jesus is nailed to the cross:

It is the sheer, unmitigated cruelty of it which disgusts us first of all. It seems unbelievable that man, created in the image and likeness of God, should be able to sink to such depths. We call such acts barbaric, inhuman.

Cruelty survives today on the grand scale – the concentration camps... the violence of modern crime... the savage cruelty of some towards their children. With me, it may be a question of motes and beams turned back to front. I am so scandalised by the viciousness of some, that I scarcely notice the speck of inhumanity in myself – my barbed wit... my lack of charity towards motorists or pedestrians... my ignoring of those I don't want to like... my willingness to gossip and say something hurtful... my condescension towards those more ignorant than myself... my impatience with those younger – or older – than myself... – pinpricks which, beside Christ's wounds, are nothing. But these are my faults, for which I am answerable.

ALL   *Help me, Jesus,*
       to heal the wounds caused by hate,
       and to show to all
       the love you have shown to me.

Prayer

NH   434

     Forget, Lord, that it was human hands
         that fashioned the wood and nails of your cross.
     Forget, too,
         that it is human hands
         that commit aggression and destruction today.
     Remember instead, Lord,
         that you are fully one of us
         and you promised to stand beside us always.
     Remember, too,

the good that has come
from the work of human hands:
    the love shared,
    the service given,
    the beauty created
    and the dignity enhanced.
As your hands were outstretched in love
    and you breathed forth your Spirit,
    so fill us with your Spirit
    that our hands may be used creatively
    and for sharing your compassion
    with our brothers and sisters. Amen.

435 Reading

St Ignatius Loyola

There are few people who realise what God would make of them if they abandoned themselves into his hands, and let themselves be formed by his grace. A thick and shapeless tree-trunk would never believe that it could become a statue, admired as a miracle of sculpture, and would never submit itself to the chisel of the sculptor, who sees by his genius, what he can make of it.

436 Prayer

Joe Seremane

1   You asked for my hands
      that you might use them for your purposes;
   I gave them for a moment and then withdrew them,
      for the work was hard.

2   You asked for my mouth
      to speak out against injustice;
   I gave you a whisper,
      that I might not be accused.

3   You asked for my eyes
      to see the pain of poverty;
   I closed them
      for I did not want to know.

4   You asked for my life
      that you might work through me;
   I gave you a small part
      that I might not get "too involved".

5   Lord, forgive me for calculated efforts to serve you
      – only when it is convenient for me to do so,

– only in those places where it's safe to do so,
– only with those who make it easy to do so.

6   Father, forgive me, renew me,
        and send me out as a usable instrument
        that I may take seriously the meaning of your Cross.

Personal Reflection

Morris West   **437**

Yesterday I met a whole man. It was a rare experience, but always an illuminating and ennobling one. It costs so much to be a full human being that there are few who have the enlightenment or the courage to pay the price… One has to abandon altogether the search for security, and reach out to the risk of loving with both arms. One has to embrace the world like a lover, and yet demand no easy return of love. One has to accept pain as a condition of existence. One has to court doubt and darkness as the cost of knowing. One needs a will stubborn in conflict, but apt always to the total acceptance of every consequence of living and dying.

Prayer

Peter de Rosa   **438**

1   Father, deepen my conviction
        that when I am weak, then I am strong.
    Too often I rely on my own gifts and capacities
        when I should rely entirely on you.

2   I believe your strength is most plainly revealed
        in the cross of Jesus Christ.
    The cross is both weakness and folly
        to those who trust in worldliness.

3   But how can I doubt, Lord, that in Christ crucified
        is your power to heal and save us?
    This is why scripture says:
    'I will lay in ruins the wisdom of the wise.
    The cleverness of the clever I will thwart.'

4   With Paul, I desire to know nothing, Father,
        except Jesus Christ and him crucified.
    What is required of us
        is that we should show others in our living and dying
        the love shown us by Jesus crucified.

5   It is difficult at first
        to stop relying on our own talents and achievements.
    But in the end, Lord, there is only peace and joy

in knowing that we cannot save ourselves,
but only deliver ourselves into your hands,
our Father and our God.

6 Help me, then, to trust you, and to boast of nothing
but the cross of our Lord Jesus Christ,
by which the world is nailed to me
and I am nailed to the world.

439 Personal Reflection

Pope John XXIII

A few days before he died in 1958, Pope John XXIII told one of his staff:

"The secret of my ministry is in that crucifix you see opposite my bed. It's there so that I can see it in my first waking moment and before going to sleep… Look at it; see it as I see it. Those open arms have been the programme of my pontificate: they say that Christ died for all – for all. No-one is excluded from his love, from his forgiveness."

440 Blessing

cf Col 2⁹

In Christ's body
lives the fullness of divinity.
May he bless us now
and bring us to fullness in him. Amen.

See also A9 in Volume 1.

Let him whisper in your ear: "I thirst for you"

Gathering in the Presence of God

Cardinal Basil Hume   **441**

It is only in the experience of praying that we become aware not only that we seek God, but that God is always seeking us.

Let us pause to remind ourselves that he is present and seeks us now.

(pause)

Reading

Catechism of the   **442**
Catholic Church

'If you knew the gift of God!' The wonder of prayer is revealed beside the well where we come seeking water: there Christ comes to meet every human being. It is he who first seeks us and asks for a drink. Jesus thirsts; his asking arises from the depths of God's desire for us. Whether we realise it or not, prayer is the encounter of God's thirst with ours. God thirsts that we may thirst for him.

Prayer

Thomas à Kempis   **443**

Trusting in your goodness and great mercy, Lord, I come:
sick – I come to my Saviour;
hungry and thirsty – to the well of life,
needy to the King of heaven

Psalm 63

Richard Gwyn OCSO   **444**

1 God, you are my God;
   my heart eagerly seeks You,
   my soul thirsts for You.

2 Parched is my body
   like a long-unwatered land
   as I await You.

3 My eyes are straining
   to see your glory light up
   the Sanctuary.

4 Your unfailing love
   is better than life itself;
   my lips will praise You.

5   So I will bless You:
    my voice raised in Your honour
    throughout all my days.

6   My soul satisfied
    as by the richest of feasts,
    I will sing Your praise.

7   Lying on my bed
    on You I muse through the night
    recalling Your help.

8   I know I am safe
    in the shadow of Your wings,
    and I sing for joy.

9   My soul clings to You
    as Your right hand holds me fast,
    ever my strong Shield.

    Glory be to the Father…

445 Reading

Cardinal Basil Hume

We each have a story, or part of one at any rate, about which we have never been able to speak to anyone. Fear of being misunderstood, inability to understand, ignorance of the darker side of our hidden lives, or even shame, make it very difficult for many people. Our true story is not told, or only half of it is.

What a relief it will be to whisper freely and fully into the merciful and compassionate ear of God. That is what God has always wanted. He waits for us to come home. He receives us, his prodigal children, with a loving embrace. In that embrace we start to tell him our story.

446 Prayer

Denis Blackledge, SJ

1   Loving Lord,
    I'm created by you
    already loved, already chosen, already befriended.
    You delight in me
    from the first moment of my human existence.
    I'm born in and for love and friendship.
    I'm born for enjoyment.
    I'm born chosen.

2   'As the Father has loved me
    so I have loved you.
    Remain in my love.'

3   All you ask of me, Lord,
    is to stay in your love,
    to just let myself be held and enfolded
    by your tender touch
    of all-embracing love.

4   And, as the song says:
    'Love changes everything'.
    Once I really do begin to let you love me
    I become an altogether new creation,
    awaking gently under your touch
    into an individual more aware and more appreciative
    of the gift that I am,
    and with a growing ability to love others around me
    whose lives I'm privileged to touch each day
    with something of the touch of love
    you have for me.

5   Now that's awesome and wonderful,
    a tremendous gift, privilege and challenge.
    'I have told you this
    so that my own joy may be in you
    and your joy be complete'.

6   Loving Lord,
    continue to whisper loudly into my mind and heart
    that message of joy.

Reading

Cardinal Basil Hume   **447**

Jesus wants to whisper a word of love into my ear. It may be a word of forgiveness, it may be a word of healing, it may be a word of comfort, it may even be a word of rebuke. He speaks to us deep down. Isn't it sad if the beloved disappoints the lover through negligence, or through walking away through stupidity?

There, in prayer at the Cross,
let him whisper in your ear:
"I thirst;
I thirst for you."

(pause)

448 Blessing

Lord Jesus,
remember us in your kingdom
and draw our hearts back to you,
that we may discover
that you do thirst for us,
and our own thirst cannot be slaked
until we find rest in you.
Bless us, we ask you,
this day and always. Amen.

"In a semblance of the gardener"

(G. K. Chesterton)

Gathering in the Presence of God

In the inspiring poetry of the Book of Genesis, we read that God walked in the garden in the cool of the evening.
We can reflect that

Gen 3[8]   **449**

> "There should be in the soul
> halls of space,
> avenues of leisure,
> and high porticos of silence
> where God walks."

Jeremy Taylor

(pause)

Let us pray:

Lord, you are not to be found
in the emptiness of the garden-tomb.
Instead, you are risen from the dead
and present with us now
as you promised to be.

NH

Reading

John 20[11-16]   **450**

1 Mary of Magdala stayed outside near the tomb, weeping. Then, still weeping, she stooped to look inside, and saw two angels in white sitting where the body of Jesus had been, one at the head, the other at the feet. They said, *"Woman, why are you weeping?"* *"They have taken my Lord away,"* she replied *"and I don't know where they have put him."*

2 As she said this she turned round and saw Jesus standing there, though she did not recognise him. Jesus said, *"Woman, why are you weeping? Who are you looking for?"* Supposing him to be the gardener, she said, *"Sir, if you have taken him away, tell me where you have put him, and I will go and remove him."*

3 Jesus said, *"Mary!"* She knew him then, and said to him in Hebrew, *"Rabbuni"* – which means Master. Jesus said to her, *"Do not cling to me, because I have not yet ascended to my Father and your Father, to my God and your God."*

4 So Mary of Magdala went and told the disciples she had seen the Lord, and that he had said these things to her.

1   Loving Lord, I want to try to put myself
        into the shoes of those individuals
        who lived through the strange privilege
        of being the first to see you really dead,
        then really risen.
    I want to feel the sort of feelings
        they surely felt.

2   Let me feel their terror
        when they went to anoint a dead body
        and were faced by angels and aliveness!
    Let me feel their fear,
        literally locked behind barricaded doors.
    Let me feel their guilt,
        knowing they'd deserted
        the one to whom they'd promised
        their friendship and their following.

3   Let me feel their joy,
        almost too much to bear,
        almost too good to be true.
    Let me feel their peace,
        your first resurrection-gift to all you meet.

4   Let me feel the overpowering sense
        of fresh freedom and future responsibilities
        written in your welcoming risen face.
    Let me feel the intimate bonding
        from the bread and breakfasting   Jn 21⁹⁻³¹
        shared with you, their risen Lord.

ALL   *Let me feel that sense of urgency*
            to spread this Good News,
            that sense of mission,
            of literally being sent by you
            to carry on your work.
        Loving Lord, let me feel the Eastering,
            as you come to meet and greet me. Amen.

Reading

G. K. Chesterton   **452**

On the third day, the friends of Christ coming at daybreak to the place, found the grave empty and the stone rolled away. In varying ways they realised the new wonder; but they hardly realised that the world had died in the night. What they were looking at was the first day of a new creation, with a new heaven and a new earth; and in a semblance of the gardener God walked again in the garden, in the cool – not of the evening – but of the dawn.

Scripture Meditation

Revelation 21$^{1-7}$ **453**

1   Then I saw a new heaven and a new earth.
    The first heaven and the first earth disappeared,
    and the sea vanished.

2   And I saw the Holy City, the new Jerusalem,
    coming down out of heaven from God,
    prepared and ready,
    like a bride dressed to meet her husband.

3   I heard a loud voice speaking from the throne:
    "Now God's home is with mankind!
    He will live with them, and they shall be his people.
    God himself will be with them, and he will be their God.

4   "He will wipe away all tears from their eyes.
    There will be no more death, no more grief or crying or pain.
    The old things have disappeared."

5   Then the one who sits on the throne said,
    "And now I make all things new!...
    I am the first and the last, the beginning and the end."

Prayer

Palestinian Women of   **454**
Jerusalem

1   O Christ,
        as we walk through the land that you loved,
        in the country where you lived and taught,
        grant us the grace and wisdom
        to see clearly and understand deeply
        that all you suffered
        was for the sake of redeeming humanity.
    Through your life, death and resurrection,
        you have made it possible for us to have life,
        and have it more abundantly.

2　O Christ,
　　　　as we follow you down the road to Calvary,
　　　　guide us to become active participants
　　　　and not curious bystanders.

3　O Christ,
　　　　as we stand with the mourners at the Cross,
　　　　give us the love
　　　　that can forgive those who trespass against us.

4　O Christ,
　　　　as we witness the new life given to us
　　　　through your Resurrection,
　　　　empower us with faith
　　　　to act and spread the Good News. Amen.

455　Blessing

cf 1 Tim 1[2]

May God the Father
and Christ Jesus our Lord
give us grace, mercy and peace. Amen.

"To know Christ and the power of his Resurrection"

Phil 3⁹

Gathering in the Presence of God

456

Recalling the words of Saint Paul, that *"It is no longer I who live, but Christ who lives in me"*, let us remind ourselves of his presence.

(pause)

Reading

Gerard Hughes, SJ   457

Christian experience confirms that we can only come to know the Risen Christ when we have undergone some kind of death, some disillusionment with ourselves and others, some loss or bereavement, some sense of fear, hopelessness or meaninglessness, and have not tried to anaesthetise ourselves against it. The answer is in the pain, which is revealing to us our poverty and our need of God.

(pause)

Prayer

Rex Chapman   458

Lord, come alive within my experience,
  within my sorrows and disappointments and doubts,
  within the ordinary moments of my life.
Come alive as the peace and joy and assurance
  that is stronger than the locked doors within,
  with which we try to shut out life.
Come alive as the peace and joy and assurance
  that nothing in life or death can kill.

Meditation

Flor McCarthy, SDB   459

1   For three long and joyous years we had followed him.
    We followed his every move.
    We drank in his every word.
    We knew neither doubt nor hesitation.

2   We were like sunflowers;
      during the day these keep turning their heads
      so that they are always facing the sun.
    But when the sun goes down
      they close their petals and hang their heads.

3 That's how it was with us.
 When the sun went down on the Master's life, we wilted.
 Without him our days lacked all charm.
 Our lives became a desert.

4 But how can we tell you
  of the joy that flooded our souls
  when we discovered that the Lord had risen?
 We cannot do so.
 Only he, by his touch,
  can do for you what he did for us,
  the day he broke through the walls
  behind which we were hiding,
  bemoaning our shattered dreams.

ALL **Risen Lord, help us to believe**
  that you are always with us,
  and that nothing in life or in death
  can separate us from you.

460 Reading

Archbishop Anthony Bloom

(writing of his student days in Paris as a convinced atheist – a period of time when "everything around seemed small and meaningless" – most reluctantly attending a meeting arranged by his youth leader: a meeting to which a priest had been invited)

1 I sat through the lecture. I didn't intend to listen… I became more and more indignant. I saw a vision of Christ and Christianity that was profoundly repulsive to me. When the lecture was over I hurried home in order to check the truth of what he had been saying. I asked my mother whether she had a book of the Gospel, because I wanted to know whether the Gospel would support the monstrous impression I had derived from his talk. I expected nothing good from my reading, so I counted the chapters of the four Gospels to be sure I read the shortest, not to waste time unnecessarily. I started to read Saint Mark's Gospel…

2 Before I reached the third chapter, I suddenly became aware that, on the other side of my desk, there was a Presence. And the certainty was so strong that it was Christ standing there, that it has never left me. This was the real turning-point. Because Christ was alive and I had been in his presence, I could say with certainty that what the Gospel said about the crucifixion of the prophet of Galilee was true, and the centurion was right when he said: "Truly he is the Son of God."

3 It was in the light of the Resurrection that I could read with certainty the story of the Gospel, knowing that everything was true in it because the

impossible event of the Resurrection was to me more certain than any event of history. History I had to believe; the Resurrection I knew for a fact...

4   I became absolutely certain within myself that Christ is alive, and that certain things existed. I didn't have all the answers, but having touched that experience, I was certain that ahead of me there were answers, visions, possibilities.

Meditation

Albert Schweitzer   **461**

> Jesus comes to us as One unknown,
>> without a name, as of old, by the lakeside.
> He came to those men who knew him not.
> He speaks to us the same word: "Follow thou me!"
>> and sets us to the tasks which he has to fulfil in our time.
> He commands.
> And to those who obey him, whether they be wise or simple,
>> he will reveal himself
>> in the toils, the conflicts, the sufferings
>> which they shall pass through in his fellowship,
>> and, as an ineffable mystery,
>> they shall learn in their own experience
>> who he is.

Blessing

Kathy Galloway   **462**

1   Our brother Jesus,
        you set our feet upon the way
        and sometimes where you lead
        we do not like or understand.

2   Bless us with courage
        where the way is fraught with dread or danger.
    Bless us with graceful meetings
        where the way is lonely.

3   Bless us with good companions
        where the way demands a common cause.

4   Bless us with night vision where we travel in the dark,
        and keen hearing where we have not sight
        so as to hear the reassuring sounds of fellow travellers.

5   Bless us with humour;
        we cannot travel lightly weighed down with gravity.

Bless us with humility
    to learn from those around us.

6   Bless us with decisiveness
    where we must move with speed.
  Bless us with lazy moments,
    to stretch and rest and savour.

7   Bless us with love,
    given and received.
  Bless us with your presence,
    even when we know it in your absence.

8   Lead us into exile
    until we find that the place where you are, is on the road,
    and you are 'going home'.

ALL   **Bless us, lead us, love us, bring us home
bearing the Gospel of life. Amen.**

"Did not our hearts burn within us?"

Emmaus
Lk 24[15]

Gathering in the Presence of God

Let us pray:

NH

After you had risen, Lord,
  two of your followers
  were walking to a village called Emmaus.
They were saddened at what had happened.
As they were talking
  you joined them on their journey
  but at first they did not recognise you.
Risen Lord,
  warm our hearts each day
  as you walk with us on life's journey
  and open our eyes now
  to recognise you in our midst.

(pause)

Prayer

Peter de Rosa

1 Father, it is strange how often
     the dearest things seem unfamiliar,
     the nearest things seem very far away.

2 On Easter Day, Jesus was not recognised
     when he walked with two of his disciples to Emmaus.
   He spoke to them and listened to them;
     and proved to them how necessary it was
     for the Christ to suffer as he was to enter his glory.
   He made them see as well
     that Calvary was all of a piece
     with Moses and the prophets.

3 Inspired by his presence, the disciples pleaded with him,
     "Stay with us, for night is coming on
     and the day is almost spent."

4 Christ, incognito, agreed and sat down with them at table.
   He assumed the role of host:
     he took the bread, blessed it, broke it
     and gave them both a share of it.
   It was through this everyday action that they knew him;
     and immediately he vanished from their sight.

5   Father, once more Christ delivers himself
        into his disciples' hands.
    In the simple gesture of the breaking of the bread
        he gives himself away;
        and though we do not see him any more,
        we believe he is always in our midst.
    His Holy Spirit is a burning presence in our hearts;
        and in our hands is broken and divided Bread.

6   Father, give us this food that will sustain us on life's journey,
        and save us from being frightened by the long and lonely night.

465 Reading

Edward Farrell

1   Everyone is on the Emmaus journey. Sooner or later Jesus catches up with
    us, and walks and talks with us as we go our way. Something usually
    prevents us from recognising him, but wherever we are and wherever we
    go, he is with us even though we cannot name why our hearts are
    smouldering within…

2   When we have been touched by Jesus, when the Spirit is stirred up in the
    depths of our being, when we dare to own Paul's words, "I live now not I,
    but Christ lives in me," then we can no longer live for ourselves alone. I
    am compelled to share my faith with others. God's presence in me
    overflows into the lives of others, and I become receptive to his presence
    and power in others…

466 Prayer

Roger Schutz, Prior of
Taizé

O Christ,
you take upon yourself all our burdens
so that, freed of all that weighs us down,
we can constantly begin anew
to walk with lightened step,
from worry towards trusting,
from the shadows towards the clear flowing waters,
from our own will
towards the vision of the coming kingdom.

And then we know,
though we hardly dared hope so,
that you offer to make every human being
a reflection of your face.

1   Miracles of beauty continually manifest God's presence:
     – I am awakened by the full moon suspended in benediction over the
     sleeping city.
     – I am lifted out of bed by the dancing of the sun on the shimmering leaves
     of the early morning breeze outside the window.

2   – I am humbled by the silence and wonder of a gentle four-year old, who
     joins in prayer for half an hour before school opens.
     – I am sustained in faith by the young man with a kidney transplant and an
     amputated leg, who affixes his crucifix to the hospital wall as a sign of the
     One who is with him.
     – I am inspired by the family who adopts their fourth handicapped child in
     gratitude for all that the Lord has given them.

3   – I am taught by the woman dying of cancer: "Don't hurry... don't talk."
     – I am in wonder at the senile person who returns to full clarity and joins
     in all the prayers in the presence of the Eucharist.

4   I sense what I call the loving companion presence through each person in
     my day. When I allow God to lift all things up with a joyful heart, I know
     the weaving of that presence among the prayer, work, frustrations and
     laughter of the day.

Prayer   *source unknown*   **468**

1   I will lift my eyes unto the hills
     to adore you.
     I will stoop down to the smallest flower
     to adore you.
     I will praise you in the stars
     when darkness falls
     And in the quiet of the night
     I will adore you.

2   I will walk among your people, Lord,
     and adore you.
     I will struggle in the market-place
     and adore you.
     I will praise you in the dust
     where blood is shed
     And in the broken hearts I find
     I will adore you.

3   I will dance among the fields in Spring
    to adore you.
    I will sing wherever children sing
    to adore you.
    I will praise you in my soul
    in stillness there,
    and for the peace you give us, Lord,
    I will adore you.

469 Blessing

NH

May the Lord Jesus give us his blessing
and cause our hearts to burn within us. Amen.

"He is going before you to Galilee"

Mark 16[7]

B24

Gathering in the Presence of God

NH   **470**

Let us pray:

cf Jn 20[19-23]

> Lord Jesus,
>> after your death
>> the doors were locked
>> in the room where your followers
>> were gathered.
>
> You appeared amongst them,
>> saying: *"Peace be with you;*
>> *receive the Holy Spirit."*
>
> As we now gather together,
>> empower us with your Holy Spirit.
>
> Bring us your peace
>> and remind us of your presence.

(pause)

Prayer

Palestinian Women of   **471**
Jerusalem

> From the land of the Resurrection
> and the cradle of the promise of salvation to all humankind
> through Jesus Christ our Lord,
> and with a candle of hope,
> we pray to you, God our Father,
> that the action of peace-seekers and peace-makers
> may bear fruit,
> so that hope will take the place of despair,
> justice will prevail over oppression,
> and peace will turn strife into love. Amen.

(pause)

Reading

Geoffrey Preston, OP   **472**

1 None of the gospel-writers really knows how to end a book properly! This is in the nature of the gospel form. The gospel form is open-ended to our living of it. The risen Jesus in St Mark goes before the disciples into Galilee. That 'going before' is part of our own theme of discipleship. The unsatisfactoriness of the ending is part of the message. *"Master, where do you dwell now?"* is one of the questions Mark expects his readers to be asking.

2 And the answer comes: *"I have gone before you into Galilee; there you will see me"*:
  – Galilee, where the disciples came from in the first place;
  – Galilee, where they had gone about their fishing or their tax-collecting or their guerilla-training just two or three years ago, the fishermen and the tax-collectors expecting to be nothing different for the rest of their working lives until, one morning, Jesus had said: *"Come, follow me"*, and their world had been turned upside down;
  – Galilee of the nations, Gentile territory, the land people looked down on and made fun of, where people spoke with outlandish accents, and had strange ideas;
  – Galilee, the world: the world as meaning 'everywhere', and world as meaning 'secular'.

3 For Mark, the disciples will see the risen Lord – not in the sphere of the 'holy', in Jerusalem – but in the sphere of the 'unholy', outside the pale. For Mark, the place where we encounter the risen Jesus is Galilee, the secular, the world which God loved, especially the non-respectable bits of it, and there you will see him – as he said! We meet Christ by dirtying our hands in the world… He is as really present in Galilee, in the world God so loved, as he is in the tabernacle.

473 Prayer Brother Roger of Taizé

    Jesus, light of our hearts,
        since your Resurrection
        you always come to us.
    Whatever point we may be at,
        you are always waiting for us.
    And you say to us:
        "Come to me, you who are overburdened
        and you will find relief."

474 Prayer Lucien Deiss

  1 Help us, O risen Lord,
      to proclaim your resurrection
      by bringing good news to the poor
      and healing the hearts that are broken.

  2 Help us, O risen Lord,
      to proclaim your resurrection
      by feeding those who are hungry
      and clothing those who are naked.

  3 Help us, O risen Lord,
      to proclaim your resurrection

by releasing the captives of injustice
and all those who are imprisoned by their sins.

4   Help us, O risen Lord,
    to proclaim your resurrection
    by welcoming the strangers
    and visiting those in loneliness.

5   Help us, O risen Lord,
    to proclaim your resurrection
    by bringing your peace to those who are in trouble
    and your joy to those who are in sorrow.

6   God our Father,
    who raised your Son from the dead,
    help us to understand, we beg you,
    that we conquer our own death
    and rise with you today
    when we live in love.

ALL   *We ask you this grace through Jesus Christ,*
        who died for our sins
        and rose for our life. Amen.

Prayer

Francis Brienen   **475**

1   God of surprises,
    when I think you are not present in my life,
    you reveal yourself in the love of friends and family
    and nurture me in your never-ending affection.

2   God of surprises,
    when we think you are not present in our community,
    you labour to make us of one heart
    and cause us to share gladly and generously.

3   God of surprises,
    when people think you are not present in our world,
    you bring hope out of despair
    and create growth out of difficulty.

4   God of surprises,
    you are ever with us.
    When the days go by and our vision fades,
    keep surprising us.

When our hope dims and our patience wears thin,
keep coming to us.

5   Teach us to keep our lamps lit
and to be prepared,
that we may see your loving presence among us.

476 Blessing   NH

Bless us, God our Father,
because you have raised Jesus, our brother, from death.
You look on us with love
and see in us the face of your Son.

Bless us, Lord Jesus,
because you are our brother.
You make our hearts burn within us.

Bless us, Holy Spirit,
because you help us to see the wonder around us.
You empower your people and pray in us. Amen.

Peter – in the light of a new dawn

Gathering in the Presence of God

Let us pray:

> Lord Jesus,
>> after you had risen,
>> you stood at the water's edge
>> as the sun was rising
>> over the Sea of Galilee.
> You asked your disciples about their fishing
>> but they were slow to recognise you.
> Lead us, gathered here,
>> to recognise that you are present,
>> standing beside us.

(pause)

Reading

Damian Lundy, FSC

1 Chapter 21 of John's Gospel… is a beautifully told story of a meeting between the risen Jesus and Simon Peter on the shore of Lake Tiberias (the Sea of Galilee). To his six companions, Peter has announced: *"I'm going fishing."* It has been suggested that these words point to a return to the way life was before Jesus disturbed it. Peter is an ex-disciple, a failure, but he is a born leader, and the others say: *"We'll come with you."* As in Luke 5, Peter is not a good fisherman, and catches nothing all night until Jesus stands at the water's edge *'when it was already light'*.

2 At the Stranger's word, the fishermen catch a hundred and fifty-three big fish – seen by many commentators as a symbol of the catholicity of the Church: it is for everyone. Then – a delightful touch – the Lord invites the disciples to *"come and have breakfast"*. The meal is described in Eucharistic terms: *'Jesus took the bread and gave it to them, and the same with the fish.'*

Prayer

Erasmus

> Lord Jesus Christ,
>> you are the sun that always rises, but never sets.
> You are the source of all life,
>> creating and sustaining every living thing.
> You are the source of all food, material and spiritual,
>> nourishing us in both body and soul.

You are the light that dispels the clouds of error and doubt,
    and goes before me every hour of the day,
    guiding my thoughts and my actions.
May I walk in your light,
    be nourished by your food,
    be sustained by your mercy,
    and be warmed by your love.

480 Reading *(continued)*

Damian Lundy, FSC

1 Eucharist is followed by reconciliation. The first thing Peter saw as he came ashore was *'some bread there and a charcoal fire with some fish cooking on it'*. The charcoal fire could not have failed to remind him of his threefold denial of Jesus, since this had taken place outside the door of the high priest's palace where *'the servants and guards had lit a charcoal fire and were warming themselves; so Peter stood there too, warming himself with the others'* (John 18:18). It was there that, when asked three times if he were not one of Jesus' disciples, he denied it three times before the cock crew…

2 A new start is needed and, after breakfast, Jesus asks Simon Peter, *"Do you love me?"* It is an emotional question, asked three times, and it is therefore an opportunity to move beyond the threefold denial to a fresh start…

3 The fact that Jesus addresses his old follower as *"Simon, son of John"* each time, is also to be noted, for John tells us that the Lord's very first words to the man he was to choose to lead his community had been, *"You are Simon, son of John"*… Now we see Jesus taking Peter back to the start of their relationship, and giving him another chance, another call. Peter's vocation will involve a change of job, from fisherman to shepherd… Peter is asked to take care of Jesus' flock, not his own. And Jesus predicts the martyr's death… The Lord then renews Peter's call to discipleship by saying: *"Follow me."*

481 Prayer

Peter de Rosa

1 Father, give us the grace to accept
    the forgiveness you keep offering us in Christ.
How often we are tempted to despair, as Judas did
    when, having betrayed Jesus with a kiss,
    he went and hanged himself.

2 This is why I marvel at Peter's humility
    for he, despite his former cowardice and apostasy,
    returned shame-faced to Christ to ask forgiveness.

3 Before Golgotha, he had boasted aloud:
    "I will die for you but not deny you, Lord",
    and then he denied him three times
    that very night before cock-crow.

4 Now, on the bank of the familiar lake,
    in the light of a new dawn,
    three times the risen Christ asked Peter pointedly:
    "Simon, son of John, do you love me?"

5 And Peter could only tell his Lord
    to look into his heart.
    "Yes, Lord," he whispered, "you know I love you."
    And Christ said: "Feed my lambs and feed my sheep."

6 Father, I praise you for the strength of Christ
    who can build his Church
    upon the rock of a weak man's faith.
    I praise you for the generosity of Christ
    who chose as his chief shepherd
    someone who deserted him
    in his hour of need.

7 Father, help me to be humble when I fail,
    and in all I do to let Christ take my arm
    and lead me wheresoever he wills.

Reading

Edward Farrell   **482**

1 The questions of Jesus are an inexhaustible revelation of his dream. *"Who do you say that I am? Do you love me? What do you want me to do for you? Do you want to be healed? Do you believe me? Do you dream? Did I not assure you that if you believed you would see the glory of God?"*

2 What did Jesus see in Peter, or James, or John or Mary Magdalene? What does Jesus see in any one of us? Over and over again, the Gospel says that Jesus knew what was in their hearts. We can be absolutely sure of but one thing: that he knows us. He knows us as we do not know ourselves.

3 What is even more important, he loves us as we cannot love ourselves, as we are worth being loved. Only Jesus has that power; he can read our depths and our heights. Jesus could look at Peter and say, *"You are Peter and upon this rock I will build my Church"*. Incredible! Imagine Jesus saying to you, *"You are the one upon whom I will build my Church."* Unbelievable as it sounds, that is what he is saying. *"Upon your marriage, upon your love for one another, I will build my community."*

4 Jesus could make wild statements about his followers, not because he was an unrealistic dreamer, but because he knows more than anyone else about the power of love. Only love creates vision; without love, there is no vision, only despair. His own heart is the power which releases in the world the tremendous reality that death no longer has any power over us.

5 No one knows more deeply than Jesus how much we are sinners, how much of us remains unredeemed. No one knows more deeply the reality of sin, our own personal sin, because he absorbed all of our sin into himself, and overcame it. That is why he has the right to love us and to have his vision for each of us.

(pause)

483 Blessing   NH

> Gathered in the presence of God the Father
> who creates us still,
> and in the love of Jesus who redeems us,
> and in the grace of the Holy Spirit who sanctifies us,
> we ask for the blessing this day and always
> of Father, Son and Spirit. Amen.

At home: the grace of your love in my ordinary, daily life

Karl Rahner

Gathering in the Presence of God

Julian of Norwich
1342-1420

484

"My good Lord opened my inward eye
and showed me my soul in the depth of my heart.
It was as big as an endless world and like a blessed kingdom.
In the middle of it sits our Lord Jesus, God and Man.
He sits in the soul in silence and peace.
And he shall never leave that place in the soul, forever.
For we are
his homeliest home
and his dwelling place for ever."

Let us remind ourselves that Jesus has, indeed, made his home in each of us.   Jn 15⁴

(pause)

Prayer

Karl Rahner, SJ

485

1 I now see clearly
   that, if there is any path at all on which I can approach you,
   it must lead through the very middle
   of my ordinary daily life.

2 If I should try to flee to you by any other way
   I would actually be leaving myself behind,
   and that, apart from being quite impossible,
   would accomplish nothing at all...

3 Your love, which can allow my daily routine
   to remain routine and still transform it
   into a home-coming to you:
   this love only you can give.

4 As I come to lay my everyday routine before you,
   there is only one thing I can beg for:
   and that is your most ordinary and most exalted gift,
   the grace of your love.

5 Touch my heart with this grace, O Lord.
   When I reach out in joy or in sorrow

for the things of this world,
grant that through them
I may know and love you,
their Maker and final home.

6 You who are Love itself,
give me the grace of love, give me yourself,
so that all my days may finally empty
into the one day of your eternal Life.

486 Reading

Edward Farrell

1 It is good to take time to be at home with myself, with the experience of solitude. There is a presence in me deeper than my own presence, a prayer, an energy, a wisdom, a connectedness, a grounding that I have only inklings of – treasure buried in a field, a pearl of great price. There is something inside of me that can receive and respond to God. He draws me. He attracts me. He fills up my life. When you want to rest, to grow, to develop: shut the door, go into your inner being. Become present to the length and breadth, the height and depth within yourself and you will learn, you will be reborn.

2 Immerse your being in God, in goodness, health and love, in beauty, joy and glory. You are God's work of art, his vineyard. There are no perfect days, yet there are perfect moments in each day. Treasure them! Treasure your connectedness with nature, with the universe, history, others, the whole world. Treasure going to the wellsprings where you are still being formed, still growing…

3 Jesus understood this rootedness, this need to be at home, when he told his disciples on the eve of his own going home to his Father: *"There are many rooms in my Father's house; if there were not I should have told you. I am going now to prepare a place for you."*

487 Prayer

Lucien Deiss

Mt 6²⁶⁻³⁰

1 You have loved our earth, Lord Jesus,
in the many-coloured flowers of the fields
more beautiful than the robe of Solomon,
and in the birds of the sky who worship the Father
by their flapping wings and their joyous chirping:
you said they are the sign of his providence!
 May you be blest, O Lord!

2 You have loved our earth, Lord,
as you admired the wedding dress of the bride.

It is beautiful, you said,
like the grace we must have
to enter the banquet of the Kingdom.
  May you be blest, O Lord!

                    Mt 22[11-12]

3 You have loved our earth, Lord,
in the street children playing their pipes and dancing,
and in the little ones brought to you in their mothers' arms.
You loved them and even embraced them.
  May you be blest, O Lord!

                    Lk 7[32]

                    Lk 18[15]

4 You have loved our earth, Lord,
in the sweet-smelling perfume, which fills the house,
and in Mary's drying your feet.
You defended her!
  May you be blest, O Lord!

                    Jn 12[3]

5 You have loved our earth, Lord,
in the lightning flash of the storm,
splitting the sky from the east to the west.
Its suddenness, you said, is a sign of the coming Kingdom
that will burst upon the world.
  May you be blest, O Lord!

                    Mt 24[27]

6 You have loved the crimson sky in the evening –
it is the throne of God, you said.
It transfigures the earth,
which you called God's footstool!
  May you be blest, O Lord!

                    Mt 16[2]

                    Mt 5[34-35]

7 You have loved our earth, Lord:
When you saw a bird's nest
you dreamed of a place to lay your head –
which you, O Son of Man, had not!
  May you be blest, O Lord!

                    Mt 8[20]

8 You have loved our earth, Lord:
you watched the budding wheat,
hurrying to grow day and night,
so as to ripen as surely as your Kingdom comes.
  May you be blest, O Lord!

                    Mk 4[26-29]

9 You have loved our earth, Lord:
you allowed yourself to be caressed by the evening breeze

                    Jn 3[8]

which wanders through the byways of Jerusalem,
as mysterious as the passing of your Spirit.
May you be blest, O Lord!

10 You have loved our earth, Lord. Rev 22[16]
When you foresaw the morning star
gleaming through the rosy light of dawn,
you thought of your own mystery –
you who are for all who seek you
the shining star of eternal morning!
May you be blest, O Lord!

488 Prayer

Bede the Venerable
672-735

O Christ, our Morning Star,
Splendour of Light Eternal,
shining with the glory of the rainbow,
come and waken us
from the greyness of our apathy
and renew in us your gift of hope.

489 Personal Reflection

Caryll Houselander

The marriage feast of the parable is here and now; and everyone has a
wedding garment if they will only accept it and put it on. Christ has laid his
humanity upon us: a seamless garment, woven by a woman, single and
complete, coloured like the lilies of the field, passing the glory of Solomon,
but simple as the wild flowers; a wedding garment worn to the shape of his
body, warm with his life.

490 Prayer

Caryll Houselander
source unknown

Be born in us, Incarnate Love.
Take our flesh and blood, and give us your humanity.
Take our lives, and give us your vision.
Take our minds, and give us your pure thought.
Take our feet, and set them in your path.
Take our hands, and fold them in your prayer.
Take our hearts, and give them your will to love.

491 Blessing

NH

May the Lord Jesus,
risen from the dead,
bless us now and always
with the joy of the new life he promises. Amen.

Gathering in the Presence of God

Let us remind ourselves that the Risen Lord of life has ascended, and is now at the right hand of the Father, praying for us. His promise is to be present with us here as we pray.

(pause)

Prayer

You are not only risen and alive, you are Lord.
This is your ascension, your ascendancy over the whole universe.
You stand over and above all that is best in life
> as its source.
You stand above all that is worst
> as ultimate victor.
You stand above all powers and authorities
> as judge.
You stand above all failure and weakness and sin
> as forgiveness and love.
You alone are worthy of total allegiance, total commitment.
You are Lord.
'My Lord and my God.'

Reading

1   If the Ascension had been Christ's departure, we would have been right to mourn and regret it. Fortunately it is nothing of the kind. Christ remains with us all days, even to the consummation of the age, but he acquires at his Ascension that boundless extension of his power that enables him to fill all things with his presence. St Paul says: "He went up to heaven in order to fill all things with his presence."

Eph 4[10]

2   We must neither bury Christ on earth nor bury him in heaven! His Ascension marks an increase of power and of effectiveness, an intensification of his presence, of which the Eucharist bears witness. It is not simply an ascension through space, which could only result in a withdrawal from us: "Do not stay here gazing up to heaven, but work on to extend his kingdom and his presence by perfecting his work here below", say the angels to the apostles.

495 Prayer

Caryl Micklem

Ascended Lord Jesus, we adore you!
Once you lived a human life
   subject to the limitations of time:
   now you are the same yesterday, today and for ever.
Once you were limited to one particular place:
   now you are present wherever people turn to you.
Once only those who met you face to face knew you:
   now your divine love extends through all the world.
Jesus, ascended Lord of time and space,
   love as wide as life,
   we adore you!

496 Personal Reflection *(continued)*

Louis Evely

St Mark mentions that *"the apostles went off and preached everywhere. The Lord worked with them and supported their preaching by the miracles which accompanied it."* What joy this is! He is here, on earth, with us, and never again will he leave us because his presence, now made spiritual, has achieved an intensity and an extension of which his physical presence would always have been incapable. It was to our advantage that he should depart in a visible manner, so that we should find him everlastingly and everywhere present in an invisible manner.

497 Prayer *(each taking a paragraph)*

Denis Blackledge, SJ

1 Loving Lord,
     our way to You echoes the way of Jesus.
  The Feast of the Ascension reminds us
     that majesty is our meaning.
  What happens to Jesus happens to each of us.

2 There is always the call to come closer,
     right into the very presence.
  Majesty evokes majesty.
  Each one of us is on Your Majesty's Loving Service.

3 Each one of us is shot through
     with those golden threads of your Son Jesus
     as we learn the way of Eastering.
  Forty days of a Lenten spring
     prepare us for the forty Resurrection days
     in the presence of you, the Majestic one,
     who conquer even death by love.

4 Loving Lord,
      help us to treasure those moments of majesty
      we feel from time to time.
  Help us on our Easter pilgrim way.
  Help us to live as Ascension people.
  Help us to celebrate our call to Majesty. Amen.

Intercessions

David Adam   **498**

1 Lord Jesus Christ, you came down to lift us up,
      you descended that we might ascend;
      grant us a glimpse of your glory.
  Give to your church a vision of your presence
      that it may proclaim your peace and your love.
      King of kings and Lord of lords,
      lift us up into your glory.

2 We pray for all who have lost vision,
      for those whose lives are clouded with doubt and fear.
  We remember those whose lives have become dull.
  May we all learn to walk in the joy of your presence.
      King of kings and Lord of lords,
      lift us up into your glory.

3 We long for the time when the kingdoms of the world
      become your kingdom.
  We pray that the peace you offer
      may be accepted by rulers and leaders;
      that all in authority may rule with gentleness but firmness.
  We pray for all who are not at peace
      with themselves or with others.
      King of kings and Lord of lords,
      lift us up into your glory.

4 We remember all who feel neglected and forsaken in our world.
  We pray for the world's poor,
      for all who are in bad housing,
      for all who live in squalor,
      for all who feel the days are dark, and that the going is rough.
      King of kings and Lord of lords,
      lift us up into your glory.

5 We give you thanks that you are with us always:
      your presence transforms our homes and our relationships.
  We bring before you the needs of our families and friends.

We pray for all who desire to improve our communities.
May those who seek to change our lives
    be people of vision.
        King of kings and Lord of lords,
        lift us up into your glory.

6 We come to you with all who are down at this time,
    may they know the power of your ascension.
In you may they find new hope and new courage.
We pray for all who are seriously ill,
    for those whose powers are waning,
    for all who cannot cope on their own.
We remember those who care for them.
Give us all a vision of your saving power.
        King of kings and Lord of lords,
        lift us up into your glory.

499 Blessing

NH

May the Lord Jesus
continue to pray for us at the right hand of the Father,
and may we live this day
in the blessing of the Father, the Son and the Holy Spirit.
Amen.

"Renew your wonders in this our day as by a new Pentecost"

Pope John XXIII

Gathering in the Presence of God

500

Let us remember that we are in the Presence of God
And let us adore him.

(pause)

Personal Reflection

Catechism of the
Catholic Church

501

There are as many paths of prayer as there are persons who pray, but it is the same Spirit acting in all and with all.

Let us ask the Spirit to fill us and pray in us today.

(pause)

Prayer

Caryl Micklem

502

Spirit of God,
    powerful and unpredictable as the wind,
    you came upon the followers of Jesus at Pentecost
    and swept them off their feet,
    so that they found themselves doing
    what they thought
    they never had it in them to do.
It is you, through all ages,
    who have fired people with enthusiasm
    to go about telling the good news of Jesus
    and serving other people for his sake.
Spirit of God,
    powerful and unpredictable as the wind,
    come upon me as I worship
    and become the driving force of my life.

Prayer

Lucien Deiss

503

*(each taking a paragraph;
everyone joining in each concluding sentence)*

  1 Holy Spirit,
     who came upon the Virgin Mary
     so that she became the Mother of Jesus,

Lk 1^{34}

we pray to you:
> **Open our hearts to your word;**
> **help us to receive Jesus, the Word of God.**

2 Holy Spirit,
who came upon Zechariah, Elizabeth, and Simeon,   Lk 1[41-67]
and helped them recognise the Messiah,   Lk 2[26]
we pray to you:
> **Enlighten the eyes of our hearts**
> **so that we may know how to recognise Jesus, the Lord.**

3 Holy Spirit,   Mt 3[16]
who came upon Christ Jesus   Mk 1[10]
when he was baptised in the waters of the Jordan,   Lk 3[22]
we pray to you:
> **Baptise us in the fire of your love**
> **so that the Father may say to each of us:**   Mt 3[17]
> **"You are my beloved Son.**   Lk 3[22]
> **On you my favour rests."**

4 Holy Spirit,   Mt 4[1]
who led out Christ Jesus   Mk 1[12]
into the desert of temptation,   Lk 4[1]
we pray to you:
> **Give us the strength**
> **to conquer in ourselves the power of evil.**

5 Holy Spirit,
who sent Christ Jesus   Mt 12[18-21]
to carry the Good News to the poor,   Lk 4[18-19]
we pray to you:
> **Help us to continue your work**
> **by serving the poor, our brothers and sisters.**

6 Holy Spirit,
who filled Christ Jesus with joy   Lk 10[21]
and opened his mouth to praise the Father,   Mt 11[27]
we pray to you:
> **Teach us to say to him,**
> **"Yes, Father, your gracious will be done!"**

7 Holy Spirit,
you who speak through the mouth of despised disciples,
we pray to you: Mt 10[20]

Place in us your words of wisdom;
help us to conquer evil by good.

Lk 13[11]
Rom 12[21]

8   Holy Spirit,
    in whom Jesus, the perfect oblation,
    is offered to the love of his Father, Heb 9[14]
    we pray to you:
       Make of us an eternal offering
       in praise of your glory. Eph 1[14]

Personal Reflection

Karl Rahner, SJ   504

1   *Let us see whether the Spirit has been at work in our own lives.*

2   Can we [ ] hough we longed to
    defend [ ] f being unjustly
    dealt wit[ ] whom nothing was
    expecte[ ] giveness simply as
    a matter [ ] t was thankless and
    unnotice[ ] isfaction? Were we
    ever a p[ ]

3   Have w[ ] vhen all emotion
    and ent[ ] emed to be uttered
    into the [ ] omless depths of a
    dreadfu[ ] en everything
    seemed [ ] eaning?

4   Did we [ ] ve could not expect
    as muc[ ] hile at the same
    time w[ ] e had acted
    unselfi[ ]

5   *Let us* [ ] *scover whether any*
    such e[ ] *I, we may be sure*
    that th[ ] *nd ourselves had a*
    brief e[ ]

Prayer

Cardinal Carlo Martini   505

1   [ ]
    that you appeared in your risen body
    to Peter and the apostles and disciples,
    and charged them anew
    with the mission of evangelisation and pastoral care.

2 We thank you
   that you sent your Spirit upon them,
   filling them with the assurance of your living presence,
   putting the right words into their mouths,
   and guiding them in times of joy and hardship.

3 We ask you, Lord,
   to show yourself in our midst with your Spirit,
   as you showed yourself in the Upper Room
   to the apostles, gathered together with Mary.

4 Put your words on our lips,
   inspire us with your intentions,
   and help us to share anew in your mission.

5 Help us to leave this place
   with a renewed awareness
   of the gift of Christian witness
   which you, in your mercy,
   have placed in our hearts,
   that many others may be drawn to you.

6 We ask this of you, Lord,
   who live and reign with the Father and the Holy Spirit
   throughout the ages. Amen.

506 Blessing   NH

Bless us, Father,
   because you love all that you have created.
Bless us, Jesus,
   because you call us your friends.
Bless us, Holy Spirit,
   because it is in you
   that we live and move and have our being. Amen.

The water I will give
will become in him
a fountain of water, bubbling up to eternal life."

5 Father, I have seen this water
   streaming from the pierced heart of Jesus crucified.
   Give me a drink of this precious water of the Spirit
   so I may never thirst again.

Personal Reflection

An African Prayer **511**
source unknown

Father, from whom all life comes,
   open wide the sluice gate into my heart
   that I may receive your living water.
Touch my heart
   that, through the power of your Spirit,
   I may grow in the new life offered in Jesus, your Son. Amen.

Prayer

Peter de Rosa **512**

1 Father, I like the abundance implied
      in the English verb *'to pour'*.
   I am impressed when rain pours down,
      when wine is poured out,
      even when insults are poured on someone's head.

2 The Psalmist exults when someone worships you, God,
      by pouring out his heart and soul.
   Isaiah honours your Suffering Servant
      because he poured out his soul to death.

3 Father, there was nothing mean or niggardly about Christ.
   He was a Man who poured himself away
      for all his brethren.
   He emptied himself so you could fill him
      with the best wine of your Spirit.

4 How could such a magnanimous man
      dispense that Spirit like a shower of rain?
   No, Father, having received from you
      the promise of the Holy Spirit,
      he poured it out on all flesh.

5 No wonder that from the day of Pentecost
      young men see visions
      and old men dream dreams.

6 Lord Jesus, pour out your Spirit on me
      like rain from an open sky,
      like water cascading down a mountain-side.

7 For only then will Isaiah's dream come true:
      my soul's desert will become a fruitful field;
      and the fruitful field
      shall seem rich as a forest, full of tall clean pines.

513 Blessing
NH

Abba, Father,
   recognise that it is your Spirit
   who prays in us,
   leading us to address you in these words.
Bless us, we ask you,
   by pouring the Holy Spirit into our hearts
   this and every day. Amen.

Gathering in the Presence of God
NH   **514**

Let us pray:

> Holy Spirit,
>> breathe new life into us
>> and fire us with enthusiasm
>> for all that is good.
> Keep in us a sense of wonder
>> at the marvels of life,
>> and lead us to be generous and wise.
> Remind us now that you are with us
>> and pray within us, we ask you,
>> as we gather in the name of Jesus. Amen.

(pause)

Reading
St Gregory of Nyssa   **515**

He did not make the heavens in his image, nor the moon, the sun, the beauty of the stars, nor any other thing you can see in the created Universe. You alone are made in the likeness of that nature which transcends all understanding. You alone are a likeness of the eternal beauty, a receptacle of happiness, an image of the true light; and if you look up to Him, you will become what He is, imitating Him who shines within you, whose glory is reflected in your purity.

Psalm 139$^{1\text{-}12}$
Richard Gwyn OCSO   **516**

1 You are watching me;
   whether I stand or sit,
   You know it at once.

2 You know all the thoughts
   of my waking or sleeping,
   and all that I do.

3 What I plan to say
   is already clear to You
   while yet unspoken.

4 You watch over me,
   keeping Your hand upon me
   at every moment.

5 Wonderful indeed
   the knowledge You have of me,
   far beyond my grasp!

6 Whither should I go
   to escape from your spirit,
   flee from Your presence?

7 Climb up to heaven?
   You are there! Sink down to hell?
   There shall I find You!

8 Travel to the east?
   Set off for western bounds?
   You would be my Guide!

9 If at my pleading
   daylight itself became dim,
   still I could not hide.

10 For to You darkness
   is as bright as the daylight,
   day and night the same.

   Glory be to the Father...

517 Reading
Edward Farrell

1 What is it to experience reverence? Have you been carried away by God? Have you had a moment of rapture, of ecstasy? Have you ever been carried away by nature? Have you ever experienced a feeling of deep reverence towards yourself? Have you ever been melted by the reverence and love of another person?...

2 Each day we all wear a new face, a face different from all the other days of our life. We need not only the time to look closely at our own faces or the faces of those we meet, we need the awareness of reverence that makes this 'deep looking' a grace and blessing, a participation in God's vision.

3 We are all called to awaken the little child within ourselves, the child who looks at the world with wonder and excitement and an unself-conscious reverence. We need that kind of reverence. For the opposite of reverence is not simply jealousy, it is violence. Not only the blatant violence of death, disease, injustice and abuse, but the subtle forms of violence –

carelessness, rejection, fear, insecurity, envy – are ways in which we fail to reverence the world around us.

4   Perhaps the saddest kind of violence is the violence we do to ourselves. We fail to appreciate, to reverence, who we are and who it is that lives in us. And insomuch as we violate the gift of the person God calls us to be, we deny others the reverence of affirming God within them. Jesus tells us that we must love God, and love our neighbours as ourselves. This demands that we first love ourselves and let ourselves be loved by God. Only then can we know what the genuine reverence of love is.

Psalm 139[13-24] *(continued)*   Richard Gwyn OCSO   **518**

1   It was You alone
     Who created my being,
     formed me in the womb.

2   It fills me with awe:
     the wonder of my being
     and of all Your works.

3   There are no secrets
     of my body and my soul
     hidden from Your gaze.

4   Your eyes beheld me
     in the intricate weaving
     that brought me to birth.

5   And into Your books
     You marked the allotted days
     that lay before me.

6   How precious to me
     are Your thoughts of me, O Lord,
     in all their vast scope!

7   To try to count them
     would be like trying to count
     sands on the seashore.

8   To finish counting
     I would have to be like You
     of age eternal!...

9 Examine me, Lord;
gaze steadily at my thoughts,
test and try my heart.

10 Never allow me
to fall into wicked ways;
keep me in Your paths.

Glory be to the Father...

519 Reading

John O'Donohue

We desperately need to retrieve our capacity for reverence. Each day that is given to you is full of the shy graciousness of divine tenderness. It is a valuable practice at night to spend a little while revisiting the invisible sanctuaries of your lived day. Each day is a secret story woven around the radiant heart of wonder. We let our days fall away like empty shells and miss all the treasure.

(pause)

520 Blessing

Ephesians 3¹⁴⁻²¹
JB

1 This, then, is what I pray,
kneeling before the Father,
from whom every family, whether spiritual or natural,
takes its name:

2 Out of his infinite glory,
may he give you the power through his Spirit
for your hidden self to grow strong,
so that Christ may live in your hearts through faith.

3 And then, planted in love and built on love,
you will with all the saints
have strength to grasp the breadth and the length,
the height and the depth,
until, knowing the love of Christ, which is beyond all knowledge,
you are filled with the utter fullness of God.

4 Glory be to him
whose power, working in us,
can do infinitely more than we can ask or imagine.
Glory be to him from generation to generation
in the Church and in Christ Jesus, for ever and ever. Amen.

A new heart and a new spirit
to be thankful in all circumstances

Gathering in the Presence of God

Let us pray:

> Holy Spirit,
>> the apostles went from strength to strength
>> once you entered their lives anew
>> and empowered them.
> Come into our lives anew
>> and pray in us
>> as we gather in the name of Jesus.

> *(pause)*

Meditation

1   I will take you from the nations
    and gather you from all the countries
    and bring you into your own land.

2   I will sprinkle clean water upon you
    and you shall be clean from all your uncleannesses,
    and from all your idols I will cleanse you.

3   A new heart I will give you,
    and a new spirit I will put within you;
    and I will take out of your flesh the heart of stone
    and give you a heart of flesh.

4   And I will put my spirit within you,
    and cause you to walk in my statutes
    and be careful to observe my ordinances.

5   You shall dwell in the land which I gave to your fathers;
    and you shall be my people,
    and I will be your God.

Prayer

> O Lord, you have mercy on all.
> Take away from me my sins
>> and mercifully set me ablaze

with the fire of your Holy Spirit.
Take away from me the heart of stone
and give me a human heart,
a heart to love and adore you,
a heart to delight in you
and to follow and enjoy you. Amen.

524 Reading

Jean Vanier

If compassion is to be a presence, it has to be made manifest by delicate signs: a letter, a phone-call, an understanding look, a discreet gift which says: "I am with you; I carry it all with you." Compassion is a hidden and discreet communication which offers hope. The distressed person is in danger of wallowing in despair and in the taste of death. The compassionate friend is there to help another continue on the road, to live this time of mourning or distress with a tiny flame of hope… Compassion is a word full of meaning. It means: sharing the same passion, sharing the same suffering, sharing the same agony; accepting into my heart the misery in yours. Your pain calls out to me; it touches my heart. It awakens something within me, and I become one with you in your pain. I may not be able to relieve your pain, but by understanding it and sharing it, I make it possible for you to bear it in a way that enhances your dignity and helps you to grow.

525 Prayer

Archbishop William Temple

All through this day, O Lord,
may we touch as many lives
as you would have us touch for you.
We ask you to enliven with your Holy Spirit
those whom we touch,
whether by the word we speak,
the letter we write,
the prayer we breathe,
or the life we live. Amen.

Personal Reflection

526 1 It is no good caring deeply for people
and concealing this behind a barrier of icy professionalism.
If people do not *know* themselves cared for,
they will be a prey to a thousand fears
of being misunderstood or rejected.

Sheila Cassidy
source unknown

527 2 People can live through great hardships
yet perish from hard feelings.

Alexander Solzhenitsyn

Prayer

Romans 12$^{9-18,21}$ **528**
NH

1 Do not let your love be a sham,
    but be sincere in choosing good rather than evil.
  Have warm affection for one another
    as brothers and sisters.

2 Be committed and enthusiastic
    as you work for the Lord,
    being happy and cheerful
    as you place your trust in him.
  Live in God's presence and keep on praying.

3 When difficulties arise, be patient.
  Set out to welcome others
    and be generous with those in need.

4 Do not curse others; bless them,
    even when they have not been good to you.
  Do all you can to live in peace with everyone.

5 Support and encourage one another,
    rejoicing with those who are happy,
    and sharing the sadness of those who are in sorrow.

6 Never look down on another person,
    but always be positive in your attitude to others.
  Be as concerned
    for those who can do nothing for you in return
    as for those who are very close to you.

7 Break the cycle of evil;
    conquer it with goodness.

Personal Reflection

Charles Dickens **529**

"Reflect upon your present blessings,
of which everyone has plenty;
not on your past misfortunes,
of which all have some."

NH

Let's pause to remember and give thanks:
    for people who have given us love and care
    and friendship and support...
    for being made who we are,

for our talents and experiences,
and for the opportunities that have come to us…

for the beauty that we can see,
for the inspiration that we have received,
and for all that has been good over the years…

for God's faithfulness and love
in good times and difficult times…

530 Blessing

Caryll Houselander

Descend, Holy Spirit of life!
Come down into our hearts – that we may live.
Descend into our emptiness – that the emptiness may be filled.
Descend into the dust – that the dust may flower.
Descend into the dark – that the light may shine in darkness.
Change our tepid nature
  into the warm humanity of Christ,
  as he changed water into wine.
Be in us a stream of life,
  as wine in the living vine.

your prudence, your reverence,
your awe, your Self!
Then Pentecost will not just be a word we utter
but an experience we daily plunge into and live.
Amen.

509 Reading

Cardinal Jean-Marie Lustiger

I delight in being able to dip my hand into a basin of holy water – beautiful, pure and fresh. It calls to mind baptismal water and the Easter Watch. Then I do not only make the Sign of the Cross *"in the name of the Father, and of the Son, and of the Holy Spirit"* but, by touching my head and chest with this water, I can recall the wealth of its symbolism which gives my life its grandeur: the first water of Creation over which the Spirit of God moved; the water of the Red Sea crossed by the Hebrews chosen to enter into a Covenant with God; the water of the River Jordan on the threshold of the Promised Land; the water of baptism; the water of tears which wash away our sins; living water that God causes to well up in us like a spring gushing forth from the Spirit.

So, when we get up in the morning, we can pray very simply: *"In the name of the Father, and of the Son, and of the Holy Spirit."*

510 Prayer

Peter de Rosa

1 Father, you contain within yourself the waters of life,
and everyone who thirsts
must come to you to drink.

2 The Psalmist wrote passionately:
*"As the deer longs for running streams,
so my soul is longing for you, my God.
My soul is thirsting for God, the living God.
When will I be allowed to see the face of God?"*

3 Again he says with equal ardour:
*"O God, you are my God, I long for you;
my soul is thirsting for you.
My body is panting for you
as in a dry, weary land without water"...*

4 On a hot midday at the well of Samaria,
Jesus said to the woman drawing from the well:
*"Everyone who drinks of this water will thirst again,
but whoever drinks of the water I will give
will never thirst.*

Gathering in the Presence of God   NH   507

Let us pray:

> Holy Spirit,
> who hovered over the waters of the earth,
> ready to turn chaos into beauty,
> lead us in our prayer
> and stir us up at this time
> to appreciate that you are in our midst,
> you in whom we live and move and have our being.
> Amen.

(pause)

Prayer   Denis Blackledge, SJ   508

1   Loving Lord,
>   just as you hovered over creation at the start,
>   so now you hover over your new creation.
>   Just as you breathed life into our first parents,
>   so now you literally inspire each one of us
>   with that gentle breeze that enlivens and enriches.

2   Loving Lord,
>   Pentecost is a constant reminder
>   that your Spirit continues to hover
>   over the chaos of your one church and one world…

3   Loving Lord,
>   let the heat of your inspiring and enfiring Spirit
>   be upon each one of us
>   so that we may truly understand
>   the treasure of your creation,
>   so that we may handle with care
>   all those whose lives we're privileged to touch
>   both near and far,
>   so that our hands and our hearts and our minds
>   may be open to receive the gifts
>   you so desperately want to give us.

4   Loving Lord,
>   don't just trickle, but pour upon us
>   your wisdom, your understanding,

Gathering in the Presence of God

531

Let us pray:

> We are children of God, called by name
> > to address him as 'Father'.
> We are invited to friendship with Jesus, our Brother,
> > who redeems us.
> We are promised the Holy Spirit, the helper,
> > who empowers us and prays within us.

As we gather to pray together, let us thank God for being present with us.

(pause)

Personal Reflection

Fr Flann Lynch OFM Cap **532**

> Father, Son and Holy Spirit,
> I adore you, I love you.
> I thank you for the wonder of my being
> and for the miracle of your presence in me.

Prayer

Lucien Deiss **533**

1 God the Father,
   we praise you and we bless you
   because you are the Father of Jesus,
   and because you wish to be our Father also
   according to your love and mercy.
   Blest are you, O Lord, through eternity!

2 God the Son,
   we praise you and we bless you
   because you are the Son of the Father's love,
   and because you wish to be the eldest brother also
   of all the children of God.
   Blest are you, O Lord, through eternity!

3 God the Holy Spirit,
   we praise you and we bless you
   because you are the love of the Father and the Son,
   springing up like a fire out of their affection,
   and because you wish to dwell in our hearts also
   like a furnace of love.
   Blest are you, O Lord, through eternity!

534 Reading

John F X Harriott

1 If we are made in the image of God, we are made in the image of the Trinity; and the life of the Trinity must in some sort be reflected in the pattern of our human life... Thus to the Father is credited all that we understand by generation, creation, maintenance; and much of our human activity can be seen as co-operation in that work...

2 Likewise all human works of compassion, healing, reconciliation, sacrifice, forgiveness, making amends and making good again, reflect the work of redemption and reconciliation identified most closely with the Son...

3 And finally the special role of the Holy Spirit is reflected in every positive idea and inspiration, however slight and humble, in every advance in knowledge and wisdom, in every flash of imagination, in every movement of the heart.

535 Prayer

Caryl Micklem

1 God the Father, God beyond us, we adore you.
       You are the depth of all that is.
       You are the ground of our being.
       We can never grasp you, yet you grasp us;
       the universe speaks of you to us,
       and your love comes to us through Jesus.

2 God the Son, God beside us, we adore you.
       You are the perfection of humanity.
       You have shown us what human life should be like.
       In you we see divine love and human greatness combined.

3 God the Spirit, God around us, we adore you.
       You draw us to Jesus and the Father.
       You are the power within us.
       You give us abundant life
       and can make us the men and women we are meant to be.

ALL   *Father, Son and Spirit;*
       God, beyond, beside and around us:
       we adore you.

Personal Reflection

Edward Farrell

In the name of the Father...

I touch my hand to my head, recognising that I share in the very intelligence of the Father, who is loving me into existence at this very moment; the Father who draws me into eternal truth and ultimate values through his eternal wisdom and order in all creation; his personal providence in my life calling me by name and giving me my daily bread.

and of the Son...

I touch my hand to my heart, remembering that Jesus will take away my heart of stone and give me a heart of flesh – knowing that he has a human heart always inviting me to learn from him, for he is gentle and humble of heart, forgiving my sins and asking me to be his healing presence for others.

and of the Holy Spirit...

I touch my shoulders leading to my hands, asking the Spirit to energise my whole body and being, that I dare to believe and hope that God's power working in me can do infinitely more than I can ask or imagine.

Amen.

Prayer
David Adam   **537**

> Blessed are you, Father, Son and Holy Spirit.
> You made the world in your love,
> you redeemed the world by your love,
> you sustain the world with your love.
> May we ever abide in your love
> and give ourselves to you in love:
> Father, Son and Holy Spirit.

Personal Reflection
Meister Eckhart   **538**
1260-1327

> Do you want to know
> what goes on at the heart of the Trinity?
> I'll tell you.
> At the heart of the Trinity
> the Father laughs, and gives birth to the Son.
> The Son then laughs back to the Father
> and gives birth to the Spirit.
> Then the whole Trinity laughs
> and gives birth to us.

Blessing
2 Cor 13[13]   **539**

> The grace of the Lord Jesus Christ,
> the love of God,
> and the fellowship of the Holy Spirit
> be with us all. Amen.

The Final Journey

Appendix

– resources for inspiration
and for accompanying the dying and those who mourn

(a) CARING ENOUGH TO TRY TO UNDERSTAND

Reading

Dame Cicely Saunders **540**

Trying to understand me

I once asked a man who knew he was dying what he needed above all from
those caring for him. He said: *"For someone to look as if they are trying to
understand me."* Indeed it is impossible to understand fully another person,
but I never forget that he didn't ask for success, but only that someone would
care enough to try.

Prayer

Mary Rosenberger **541**

Colours and maturity of Autumn

Master Painter,
as the days grow short
and the chill winds blow,
you colour the trees more beautifully every day,
brushing the leaves with brilliant hues
of reds and golds until
suddenly and quietly they fall.

And our lives should be like that, too, I think,
for, as the days grow short,
and the bones begin to chill,
you colour our days with the brilliant hues
of experience and wisdom,
but we –
we miss the beauty and see only the fall,
for, by worshipping the fleeting youth of spring
we have become blinded to the deep beauty of autumn!

(b) ABOUT DYING

Reading

Peter O'Ryan **542**

Terminal illness but a fulfilling life

...In 1994 I was diagnosed as having a problem with my lower neurones.
Since then I have become much weaker. It is now thought that I have an

atypical form of motor neurone disease. It is unlikely that I will live to this autumn, which gives another meaning to my reaching retirement age. My breathing will give out because my intercostal muscles will become so weak.

I have had a wonderfully fulfilling life. But I have made some terrible mistakes and I have let people down that I love, and myself. While I would love to keep on living, that is not to be. In fact I think my motor neurone disease is one of the most joyous happenings of my life. How can this be? The cost, a heavy one, is totally outweighed by all the love I have received and been able to give. I would never have received it without my disease. I have been so enlightened! And when I say 'love' I mean not just from my family, but from the staff of the NHS, the social services and many total strangers. Among those strangers is Jesus Christ, whom I thought I knew until the chips were really down. I have come into *his* own!

I get very upset at the thought of leaving my wife, family, friends and everybody else. I am rather afraid of the actual process of dying. But the thought of being in the Presence fills me with excitement and joy…

543 Prayer

Blaise Pascal

All things can be channels of your compassion
Lord, you are good and gentle in all your ways,
    and your mercy is so great
    that not only the blessings
    but also the misfortunes of your people
    are channels of your compassion.
Grant that I may turn to you as a Father
    in my present condition,
    since the change in my own state from health to sickness
    brings no change to you.
You are always the same,
    and you are my loving Father
    in times of trouble and in times of joy alike.

544 Prayer

A Muslim prayer

The best
Lord, may the end of my life
    be the best part of my life.
May my closing acts
    be my best acts,
    and may the best of my days
    be the day when I shall meet you.

Reading

Like homesick birds returning home
Like a flock of homesick cranes flying night and day back to their mountain nests, let all my life take its voyage to its eternal home in one salutation to thee.

Reading

Dying: going home
People ask me about death and whether I look forward to it, and I answer, "Of course", because I am going home. Dying is not the end, it is just the beginning. Death is a continuation of life. This is the meaning of eternal life; it is where our soul goes to God, to be in the presence of God, to see God, to speak to God, to continue loving him with greater love – because in heaven we shall be able to love him with our whole heart and our soul because we only surrender our body in death – our heart and our soul live forever.

When we die we are going to be with God, and with all those we have known who have gone before us; our family and our friends will be there waiting for us. Heaven must be a beautiful place.

Reading

God waits at home for our return
Travelling – seeing new sights, hearing new music, and meeting new people – is exhilarating. But when we have no home to return to where someone will ask us, "How was your trip?" we might be less eager to go. Travelling is joyful when we travel with the eyes and ears of those who love us, who want to see our slides and hear our stories. This is what life is about. It is being sent on a trip by a loving God, who is waiting at home for our return, and is eager to watch the slides we took and hear about the friends we made. When we travel with the eyes and ears of the God who sent us, we will see wonderful sights, hear wonderful sounds, meet wonderful people… and be happy to return home.

Reading

God waits for me to come home and tell my story
I still believe deeply that our few years on this earth are part of a much larger event that stretches out far beyond the boundaries of our birth and death. I think of it as a mission into time: a mission that is very exhilarating and even exciting, mostly because the One who sent me on the mission is waiting for me to come home and tell the story of what I have learned.

549 Reading

Cardinal Basil Hume

We tell God our story

We each have a story, or part of one at any rate, about which we have never been able to speak to anyone. Fear of being misunderstood, inability to understand, ignorance of the darker side of our hidden lives, or even shame, make it very difficult for many people. Our true story is not told, or only half of it is.

What a relief it will be to whisper freely and fully into the merciful and compassionate ear of God. That is what God has always wanted. He waits for us to come home. He receives us, his prodigal children, with a loving embrace. In that embrace we start to tell him our story... I now have no fear of death. I look forward to my deceased friend leading me to a world where I shall know God and be known by him as his beloved child.

550 Reading

Oliver Hall
source unknown

Somebody helps us over the stile; then a door will open

I have no fear of death – but I shall welcome a helping hand to see me through. For it is said that just as everyone has a guardian angel, so to each one comes somebody to help us over the stile. Once I am over, I know a door will open on a new loveliness and freshness of colour, form and light, which is far more beautiful than anything I have ever seen or imagined.

551 Reading

Mother Teresa

How much love put into the doing

When you die, the Lord will not ask you
how much you have done with your life,
but how much love you have put into the doing.

552 Reading

Thornton Wilder

A bridge of love between the living and the dead

Soon we shall die... and we shall be loved for a while and forgotten. But the love will have been enough; all those impulses of love return to the love that made them. Even memory is not necessary for love. There is a land of the living and a land of the dead, and the bridge is love, the only survival, the only meaning.

553 Reading

John Magee

Touched the face of God

Number 104 in Volume 1 of *Walk In My Presence* is the poem, *"Oh I have slipped the surly bonds of earth... and touched the face of God"*, by John Magee, an RAF pilot killed in 1941.

Reading

Canon Henry Scott-Holland
1847-1913

554

Death is slipping away

Death is nothing at all,
  I have only slipped away into the next room.
I am I, and you are you –
  whatever we were to each other, that we are still.

Call me by my old familiar name.
Speak to me
  in the easy way which you always used.
Put no difference into your tone.
Wear no forced air
  of solemnity or sorrow.
Laugh as we always laughed
  at the little jokes we enjoyed together.
Play, smile, think of me, pray for me.
Let my name be ever the household word it always was.
Let it be spoken without effect,
  without the ghost of a shadow on it.
Life means all that it ever meant.
It is the same as it ever was;
  there is absolutely unbroken continuity.

What is this death but a negligible accident.
Why should I be out of mind
  because I am out of sight?
I am but waiting for you, for an interval,
  somewhere very near,
  just around the corner.
All is well.

Reading

Victor Hugo

555

Dying; ship over the horizon

What is dying?
The ship sailed away
  and I stand watching till it fades on the horizon
  and someone at my side says: "The ship is gone."
Gone where? Gone from my sight, that is all;
  the ship is just as large as when I saw it.
As I see the ship grow smaller and go out of sight
  it is just at that very moment
  that there are others in a different place who say:
"Watch; here the ship comes",

and other voices take up a glad shout:
"You have arrived"
  – and that is what dying is about.

556 Reading

Minnie Louise Haskins

Put your hand into the hand of God
I said to the man who stood at the gate of the Year:
  "Give me a light
  that I may tread safely into the unknown."
And he replied:
  "Go out into the darkness
  and put your hand into the hand of God.
  That shall be to you
  better than light,
  and safer than a known way."
May that almighty hand
  guide and uphold us all.

557 Reading

Henri J.M.Nouwen

Stretch out your arms and trust
*The author tells of 'The Flying Rodleighs', trapeze artists in a German
circus, and he reflects on a conversation with them:*
One day I was sitting with Rodleigh, the leader of the troupe, in his caravan,
talking about flying. He said: "As a flyer I must have complete trust in my
catcher. You and the public might think that I am the great star of the trapeze,
but the real star is Joe, my catcher. He has to be there for me with split-second
precision, and grab me out of the air as I come to him in the long-jump!"
"How does it work?" I asked him. Rodleigh said, "The secret is that the flyer
does nothing and the catcher everything! When I fly to Joe, I have simply to
stretch out my arms and hands, waiting for him to catch me and pull me
safely over the apron behind the catchbar."

"You do nothing?" I said, quite surprised. "Nothing," Rodleigh repeated. "The
worst thing the flyer can do is to try to catch the catcher. I am not supposed
to catch Joe. It's Joe's task to catch me. If I grabbed Joe's wrists, I might break
them, or he might break mine, and that would be the end for both of us! A
flyer has to fly, and a catcher has to catch; and the flyer has to trust with
outstretched arms, that his catcher will be there for him!"

When Rodleigh said this with so much conviction, the words of Jesus flashed
through my mind: "Father, into your hands I commend my spirit" (Lk 23[46]).
Dying is trusting in the Catcher! Caring for the dying is saying: "Don't be
afraid, remember you are a beloved child of God. He will be there when you

make your long jump… don't try to catch him, he will grab you… just stretch out your arms and hands, and trust, trust, trust.

Reading
Pedro Arrupe, SJ   558

Into the arms of the Lord
Is death a leap into a void? Of course not. It is to throw yourself into the arms of the Lord.

(c) DYING

Prayer
George Appleton   559

Links grow weaker; beginning the journey
1   There will come a time, O Lord,
    when my links with earth grow weaker,
    when my powers fail;

2   when I must bid farewell to dear ones
    still rooted in this life
    with their tasks to fulfil
    and their loved ones to care for;
    when I must detach myself from the loveliest things
    and begin the lonely journey.

3   Then I shall hear the voice
    of my beloved Christ, saying,
    "It is I; be not afraid."

4   So, with my hand in his,
    from seeming dark valley
    I shall see the shining City
    and climb with trusting steps
    and be met by the Father of souls
    and clasped in the everlasting arms.

Reading
Rabindranath Tagore   560

I am ready for my journey
I have got my leave. Bid me farewell. I bow to you all and take my departure. Here I give back the keys of my door – and I give up all claims to my house. I only ask for last kind words from you. We were neighbours for long, but I received more than I could give. Now the day has dawned and the lamp that lit my dark corner is out. A summons has come, and I am ready for my journey.

561 Prayer

St Teresa of Avila

Time to move on

My Lord, it is time to move on.
Well then, may your will be done.
O my Lord and my Spouse,
    the hour that I have longed for has come.
It is time for us to meet one another.

562 Prayer

Luke 2$^{29\text{-}31}$

You give me leave to go in peace

At last, all powerful Master,
    you give leave to your servant
    to go in peace, according to your promise.
For my eyes have seen your salvation.

563 Prayer

St Clare of Assisi
about to die, speaking
to herself

It is now safe for your journey

Go now; it is quite safe to leave,
    for you have a good guide for the journey.
Go now, for he who created you
    has also made you holy.
He has always kept you safe
    and loved you with a tender love,
    as a mother loves her child.

564 Prayer

Charles de Foucauld

Into your hands

Father, I abandon myself into your hands;
    do with me what you will.
Whatever you may do, I thank you.
I am ready for all, I accept all;
    let only your will be done in me,
    and in all your creatures.
I wish no more than this, O Lord.
Into your hands I commend my soul
    and offer it to you with all the love of my heart;
    for I love you, Lord,
    and so need to give myself,
    to surrender myself into your hands without reserve,
    and with boundless confidence,
    for you are my Father.

Committal (addressing the one who is dying)

Jesus welcomes and presents you to the Father
The Lord Jesus ascended into heaven,
where he now sits at the right hand of the Father,
praying for you.
May Jesus who called you to follow him
now take you by the hand
and present you to our Father
who has written your name
on the palm of his hands.

A Song of Farewell

Accompanying the dying
1   Go forth, ***N***, upon your final journey.
    Go from this world and rest in peace
        in the presence of God the Father, who created you;
        in the love of Jesus our Lord, who calls you his friend,
        and in the warmth of the Holy Spirit,
        who has made his home in you.

2   In death
        your life is changed, not ended,
        and we give you back to our faithful God
        who first gave you to us.
    On our common pilgrimage
        we have accompanied you
        as far as we can go together.
    Our ways part for now
        but, beyond our horizon,
        you will be met by Jesus
        who is himself the Way.

3   May the angels lead you into paradise,
        and the saints take you by the hand
        and walk with you into the presence of God.

4   There, face-to-face, you will meet our loving Father.
    His hands will be swift to welcome,
        and he will hold you close:
        his tender love
        is that of a mother for her child,
        and he has written your name, ***N***,
        on the palm of his hands.

5   You will find rest
        in Christ, the Good Shepherd,
        who carries you and says: "Do not be afraid."
    His peace will be yours
        in a place where pain and sorrow will be no more.

6   There in God's kingdom
        of light, happiness and peace
        the Holy Spirit will heal and renew
        and strengthen you.

7   The end of your pilgrimage
        will be a new beginning
        in the bright dawn of eternal day.

8   Go forth, **N**, upon your final journey.
    Go from this world, and be with God.

(This Song of Farewell can be used in accompanying the dying, or be recited by one or more family members or friends at the funeral. Paragraphs 3 and 8 could be recited together by several people.)

567 Prayer

Attributed to William Penn and also to others; the prayer is not by Bede Jarrett

We give them back to you, O Lord

1   We give them back to you, O Lord,
        who first gave them to us;
        and as you did not lose them in the giving,
        so we do not lose them in the return.

2   Not as the world gives do you give,
        O Lover of souls.
    For what is yours is ours also
        if we belong to you.

3   Life is unending because love is undying,
        and the boundaries of this life
        are but an horizon,
        and an horizon is but the limit of our vision.

4   Lift us up, strong Son of God,
        that we may see further.
    Strengthen our faith
        that we may see beyond the horizon.

5   And while you prepare a place for us
        as you have promised,
        prepare us also for that happy place,
        that where you are, we may be also,
        with those we have loved, forever.

Prayer 568

Hold them in your love
Loving Father,
    to you the dead do not die
    and, in death, our life is changed – not ended.
We believe that all that binds us together
    in love and friendship
    does not end with death.
Hear our prayers for **N** who has died.
As you have made each of us
    in your image and likeness
    and have called us by name,
    hold **N** in your love
    in your kingdom of light, happiness and peace.

(d) MOURNING

Prayer Jewish prayer 569

In the hands of God; praying for those who mourn
To complete the work of God in this world is not given to anyone, for even if we work with all our strength, the result is in the hands of God. May those who mourn be comforted, for the Lord is faithful to all his creatures, and his love is constant for all eternity.

Prayer NH 570

Only those who love greatly can mourn
Lord Jesus, you tell us
    that those who mourn are blessed,
    knowing that only those who love greatly
    can mourn.
We know, too,
    that it is better to have loved and lost someone
    than never to have loved at all.
May **N's** family
    find strength and peace
    through the support and kindness of others,
    knowing that other people care for them
    and hold them in prayer. Amen.

571 **Reading**

H.M. Queen Elizabeth II

Grief and love

Grief is the price we pay for love.

572 **Reading**

H.M. Queen Elizabeth,
the Queen Mother

Getting better at it

No, it doesn't get any better, but you do get better at it.

573 **Prayer**

NH

Healing and peace for those mourning

Father,
    bring courage and strength
    to those who now mourn
    because they have loved greatly.
In your loving kindness
    bring them healing and inner peace,
    and lead the one they mourn
    into your kingdom
    of light, happiness and peace.

574 **Prayer**

Michael Walker

Day-to-day difficulties

Lord,
    as the numbness passes
    the pain gets sharper.
I expect to hear a familiar voice.
I walk into a room,
    see an empty chair
    and can hardly hold back the tears.
I turn to share something,
    an item of news, an anxiety,
    something I saw when I was out,
    and there is no-one to share it with.
I don't want to be eaten up with self-pity
    but, Lord, I need your pity.
I'm not asking to be brave,
    just to survive this awful emptiness – this grief.
They tell me that one day the pain will get easier,
    one day I will finally be able to let go.
That day hasn't come yet, Lord.
Until then, let me know that you are near me.

Prayer

Certainty that the loved one is with the Lord
Lord God,
 … look in pity on those who mourn.
Make your loving presence so real to them
 that they may feel round about them
 your everlasting arms,
 upholding and strengthening them.
Grant them such a sense of certainty
 that their loved one is with you,
 doing your service, unhindered by pain,
 that they may turn to life's tasks
 with brave hearts and steady nerves,
 consoled in the thought
 that they will meet their dear one again.
Teach us all to face death unafraid
 and take us at last in triumph through the shadows
 into your everlasting light
 where there will be reunion and never-ending joy. Amen.

Prayer

Gratitude for my beloved
Loving Lord,
 give me, give all who grieve,
 a sense that the best is yet to come,
 a sense of gratitude for all the past,
 a sense of openness to all that is to be,
 a sense of aliveness in the present moment
 and, in all the love-pain,
 a deep-felt gratitude for my beloved. Amen.

Blessing

A safe lodging
May the Lord support us all the day long,
 till the shades lengthen and the evening comes
 and the busy world is hushed,
 and the fever of life is over
 and our work is done.
Then, in his mercy,
 may he give us a safe lodging and a holy rest,
 and peace at the last. Amen.

Hymns

ADVENT

B1

Come let us go up to the Lord
Come, Lord Jesus, come
How lovely on the mountains
Now watch for God's coming
O come, O come, Emmanuel
The day of the Lord shall come
Word made flesh, Son of God

B2

Come let us go up to the Lord
Comfort, comfort, O my people
O comfort my people
O come, O come, Emmanuel
Now watch for God's coming
The day of the Lord shall come

B3

Creator of the stars of night
Hail Mary
Holy Virgin, by God's decree
Mary most holy
Mother of God's living word
My soul is filled with joy
My soul proclaims the Lord, my God
My soul proclaims you, mighty God
Oh Mary, when our God chose you
Sing of a girl in the ripening wheat
Tell out my soul
The Angel Gabriel
When Mary listened to God's word
When the angel came to Mary
Word made flesh, Son of God

B4

A voice cries out in the wilderness
Blest be the Lord, the God of Israel
Come, Lord, to a world of longing
God has chosen me

Hark a herald voice is calling
O comfort my people
On Jordan's bank
Our God reigns (How lovely on the mountains)
Wait for the Lord (Taizé)

CHRISTMAS

B5

A child is born for us today
Away in a manger
City of God (Awake from your slumber)
Creator of the stars of night
I saw springs of water flowing from the temple
O come, all ye faithful
O little town of Bethlehem
Praise to you, O Christ our Saviour, Word of the Father
Silent night
The light of Christ

B6

Adoramus te, Domine (Taizé)
Hark the herald angels sing
In deepest night we hear the story
Jesus the Word has lived among us
O come, all ye faithful
Oh the word of my Lord
Praise to you, O Christ our Saviour, Word of the Father
Silent night

B7

A child is born for us today
Adoramus te, Domine (Taizé)
Angels we have heard in heaven
Away in a manger
Come, come, come to the manger
God rest ye merry gentlemen
Go, tell it on the mountain
In the bleak midwinter
O come, all ye faithful
Once in royal David's city

Silent night
While shepherds watched

B8

A child is born for us today
Angels we have heard in heaven
Away in a manger
God rest ye merry gentlemen
Hark the herald angels sing
In the bleak midwinter
O come, all ye faithful
Once in royal David's city
Praise to you, O Christ our Saviour, Word
Silent night
While shepherds watched

B9

God is working his purpose out
Lord, for the years your love has kept
The God of all eternity

B10

As with gladness men of old
Come and join the celebration
In the bleak midwinter
Songs of thankfulness and praise
The first nowell
We three kings of orient are
What child is this, who laid to rest

LENT

B11

Bless the Lord, my soul (Taizé)
Come back to me, with all your heart
Dear Lord and Father of mankind
Forty days and forty nights
Freely, freely (God forgave my sin)
Lay your hands
Lord Jesus think on me
O Lord, be not mindful of our guilt
Turn to me
We rise again from ashes

B12

Bless the Lord, my soul (Taizé)
Come back to me, with all your heart
Dear Lord and Father of mankind
Freely, freely (God forgave my sin)
In you, my God, may my soul
Lay your hands
O let all who thirst
O Lord, all the world belongs to you
O Lord, be not mindful of our guilt
Praise to you, O Christ our Saviour, Word of the Father
Though the mountains may fall
Turn to me

B13

Be still for the presence of the Lord
How good, Lord, to be here
Jesus take me as I am
This is holy ground, we're standing on holy ground
We behold the splendour of God

B14

All that I am, all that I do
Darkness falls, my hour has come
Into one we all are gathered
Let all mortal flesh keep silence
Lord Jesus Christ, upon the night
Love is his word
Make us one, Lord
O Lord, all the world belongs to you
One bread, one body
One cold night in Spring
The night before our Saviour died
This is my will, my one command
Ubi Caritas (Taizé)
Where is love and loving kindness

B15

Be not afraid
Darkness falls, my hour has come
Do not be afraid
Stay with me, remain here with me (Taizé)

B16

Because the Lord is my shepherd
Blest be the Lord (He will release me)
Brother, Sister, let me serve you (Servant Song)
Come, come, follow me
Come, my Way, my Truth, my Life (The Call)
Fight the good fight
Follow me
He who would valiant be
Jesus, you are Lord (I am the way)
Lead kindly light
Lord, make me a means of your peace
Make me a channel of your peace
O Christe Domine Jesu (Taizé)
Walk with me, O my Lord

B17

Blest be the Lord (He will release me) - *sung slowly*
Jesus, remember me (Taizé)
O Christe Domine Jesu (Taizé)
One cold night in Spring
The Lord hears the cry of the poor

B18

Abba, Father, from your hands
O Christe Domine Jesu (Taizé)
O Lord, your tenderness, melting all my bitterness
One cold night in Spring
Without beauty, without majesty we saw him

B19

In him we knew a fullness
Jesus, remember me (Taizé)
Lord, make me a means of your peace
O Christe Domine Jesu (Taizé)
One cold night in Spring
O sacred head ill-used
Take my hands

B20

Abba, Father, from your hands
The love I have for you, my Lord (Only a shadow)
Your love is finer than life

EASTER

B21

Christus resurrexit (Taizé)
Morning has broken
New daytime dawning
Now the green blade riseth
You who sleep, rise up, alleluia

B22

Christus resurrexit (Taizé)
Come, come, follow me
Follow me
For to those who love God
For you are my God
Jesus, you are Lord (I am the Way)
Keep in mind
You who sleep, rise up, alleluia

B23

Adoramus te, Domine (Taizé)
Alleluia, alleluia, give thanks to the risen Lord
Are not our hearts burning within us?
Did not our hearts burn within us?
For to those who love God
For you are my God
On the journey to Emmaus
Sing of one who walks beside us

B24

Alleluia, alleluia, give thanks to the risen Lord
Forth in the peace of Christ we go
For to those who love God
For you are my God
Freely, freely (God forgave my sin)
Go to the world! Go into all the earth!
Here I am, Lord (I, the Lord of sea and sky)
If God is for us
I heard the Lord call my name
Jesus, you are Lord (I am the way)
Keep in mind
We are the Easter People

B25

All heav'n declares the glory of the risen Lord

Be thou my vision

Christ is alive, with joy we sing

Colours of Day (Light up the fire)

I watch the sunrise

I will be with you wherever you go

Lay your hands

New daytime dawning

On eagle's wings (You who dwell in the shelter of the
   Lord)

The light of Christ

B26

Christ is alive, with joy we sing

Christus resurrexit (Taizé)

Do not **worry over** what to eat

Forth in thy name, O Lord, I go

God beyond all names

In your coming and going God is with you

Join in the **dance of the earth's jubilation**

Look and learn from **the birds of the air**

Lord of all hopefulness

O the love of my Lord is the essence

The love I have for you

You who sleep, rise up, alleluia

B27

Abba, Father, send your Spirit

Be still and know I am with you

Darkness falls, my hour has come

Go to the world! Go into all the earth!

Majesty

New praises be given

Sing to the world of Christ our sov'reign Lord

SPIRIT

B28

Abba, Father, send your Spirit

Breath of God, O Holy Spirit

Come down, O love divine

Holy Spirit, we welcome you

Shine, Jesus, shine

Veni Sancte Spiritus (Walker)

B29

Abba, Father, from your hands

Abba, Father, send your Spirit

Breath of God, O Holy Spirit

God, whose almighty Word

O living water

The light of Christ

B30

Breath of God, O Holy Spirit

Come, Holy Spirit, fill the hearts of your faithful

Oh the word of my Lord

O the love of my Lord is the essence (As gentle as
   silence)

The Holy Spirit has come down

The love I have for you

This, then, is my prayer (Ephesians 3)

Yahweh is the God of my salvation

B31

Abba, Father, **send your** Spirit

All that I am, all **that I** do

A new comman**dment**

Come down, O love divine

Go to the world! Go into all the earth!

Grant to us, O Lord, a heart renewed

Holy Spirit, we welcome you

O the love of my Lord is the essence (As gentle as
   silence)

Spirit of truth and grace

The Holy Spirit has come down

This is my will, my one command

B32

All people that on earth do dwell

Come, praise the Lord, the Almighty

Father, in my life I see

Father, Lord of earth and heaven

God, whose almighty Word

Great God of mercy, God of consolation

How great is our God

I bind unto myself today

Lead us, heav'nly Father, lead us

This day God gives me

Sources

'NH' against a text indicates authorship by Nicholas Hutchinson, FSC

302   Lucien Deiss *'Come Lord Jesus'*, based on the seven *'O' Antiphons*, pg 119, World Library Publications

303   Ann Wroe *'The Tablet'*, 18 Dec 1999

304   Karl Rahner *'Encounters with Silence'*, pg 79, Burns & Oates, 1975

308   David Adam *'Tides and Seasons'*, pg 26, Triangle/SPCK

313   Denis Blackledge, SJ *'Loving Lord: Encounters'*, pg 11

314   Edward Farrell *'Gathering the Fragments'*, pg 75, Ave Maria Press, USA

315   Terence Collins FSC

317   Peter de Rosa *'Bible Prayer Book for Today'*, pg 96, Collins Fount

318   Lucien Deiss *'Come Lord Jesus'*, pg 198, World Library Publications

325   Michael Campbell-Johnston, SJ *'The Tablet'*, 14 Aug 99

330   Dietrich Bonhoeffer (1906-1945), written while awaiting execution in a Nazi prison, *'Letters and Papers from Prison'*, SCM Press

332   Henri Nouwen *'The Genesee Diary'*, DLT

333   Ray Simpson *'Celtic Worship through the Year'*, pg 23, Hodder & Stoughton

334   *'The Tablet'*, 11 Sept 1999, about Cardinal Basil Hume

337   Henri Nouwen *'Lifesigns'*, Doubleday, Random House

338   Michael Hollings, a paraphrase of the Roman Missal's Opening Prayer of the Dawn Mass of Christmas Day

339   Oscar Romero *'The Violence of Love'*, HarperCollins

340   Kathy Galloway *'The Pattern of our Days'*, Wild Goose Publications, 1996

341   John Powell *'The Christian Vision'*, Argus Communications

342   Karl Rahner *'Kleines Kirchenjahr'*, Muenchen: Ars Sacra, 1954, pg 15-19

345   Oscar Romero *'The Promise of Peace'*, Pax Christi, 1998

347   Mark Link, SJ *'Take off your Shoes'*, Argus Communications

348   Denis Blackledge, SJ *'Loving Lord: Seasons'*, pg 15, Sanctuary Books, Preston

349   Donal Neary, SJ *'The Calm Beneath the Storm'*, pg 42, Veritas

351   Denis Blackledge, SJ *'Loving Lord: Moments'*, pg 24, Sanctuary Books, Preston

352   David Konstant *'Jesus Christ, the Way, the Truth and the Life'*, pg 94, Collins

353   Geoffrey Preston, OP *'God's Way to be Man'*, pg 23, DLT

355   Edward Farrell *'Free to be Nothing'*, pg 102, Liturgical Press, Collegeville, Mn, USA

356   Catherine Moran, HFB; the final paragraph is inspired by a prayer of the Roman Missal

359   Frank Topping *'Pause for Thought with Frank Topping'*, pg 71, Lutterworth Press

360   Francis Brienen *'A Restless Hope'*, United Reformed Church, 86 Tavistock Place, London WC1H 9RT

361   Minnie Louise Haskins, quoted by King George VI in his Christmas Day Broadcast, 1939, whilst Britain then stood alone against Nazi Germany in the first months of the Second World War

362   Denis Blackledge, SJ *'Loving Lord: Seasons'*, pg 20, Sanctuary Books, Preston

365   John O'Donohue *'Eternal Echoes'*, pg 280, Bantam Books

366   Denis Blackledge, SJ *'Loving Lord: Seasons'*, pg 26, Sanctuary Books, Preston

368   Lucien Deiss *'Come Lord Jesus'*, pg 139, World Library Publications

369   W. H. Auden *'For the Time Being'*

370   David Adam *'Traces of Glory: Prayers for the Church Year (B)'*, pg 23, SPCK

373 Peter de Rosa *'Bible Prayer Book for Today'*, pg 108, Collins Fount

375 Frank Topping *'Wings of the Morning'*, pg 16, Lutterworth Press

376 Anthony Padovano *'Dawn Without Darkness'*, Doubleday Image, USA, 1971

377 This anonymous prayer was written on a piece of wrapping-paper and was found beside a dead body in Ravensbruck Concentration Camp, where 92,000 women and children were killed.

380 Flann Lynch OFM Cap, Dublin Street, Carlow, Ireland

381 Frank Topping *'Pause for Thought with Frank Topping'*, pg 189, Lutterworth Press

382 Anthony Bloom *'Living Prayer'*, pg 115, DLT, 1966

383 Lucien Deiss *'Come Lord Jesus'*, pg 145, World Library Publications

384 Michael Mayne *'Pray, Love, Remember'*, pg 46, DLT

386 Mark Link, SJ *'Path through Catholicism'*, pg 178, RCL, Allen, Texas, USA

389 Peter de Rosa *'Bible Prayer Book for Today'*, pg 31, Collins Fount

390 Denis Blackledge, SJ *'Loving Lord: Encounters'*, pg 52, Sanctuary Books, Preston

392 John O'Donohue *'Eternal Echoes'*, adapted from the second person plural to the third, pg 260, Bantam Books

394 Sister Briege McKenna *'Miracles Do Happen'*, pg 58, first published by Veritas Publications

395 C I Pettitt *'A One Hour Service for Good Friday'*, SPCK, 1973

396 Sister Briege McKenna *'Miracles Do Happen'*, pg 58, first published by Veritas Publications

398 Edward Farrell *'Free to be Nothing'*, pg 84, Liturgical Press, Collegeville, Mn, USA

400 Abridged from Dom Gregory Dix *'The Shape of the Liturgy'*, A & C Black, 1945

402 Hugh Kay *'The Way'*

403 Denis Blackledge, SJ *'Loving Lord: Moments'*, Sanctuary Books, Preston

406 Reinhold Neibuhr *'The Serenity Prayer'*

407 Sister Helen Prejean, CSJ *'Dead Men Walking'*, pg 104, HarperCollins

408 Peter de Rosa *'Bible Prayer Book for Today'*, Collins Fount

409 John O'Donohue *'Eternal Echoes'*, pg 237, Bantam Books

414 *'Rule for a New Brother'*, pg 8, Blessed Sacrament Fathers, Brackenstein, DLT

417 Dietrich Bonhoeffer *'The Cost of Discipleship'*, translated by R H Fuller, pg 162, SCM Press, 1956

420 Donal Neary, SJ *'Masses with Young People'*, pg 40, Columba Press

421 Peter de Rosa *'Bible Prayer Book for Today'*, pg 50, Collins Fount

424 Sheila Cassidy *'Good Friday People'*, DLT, 1991

427 David Konstant *'Jesus Christ, the Way, the Truth and the Life'*, pg 106, Collins

428 Lucien Deiss *'Come Lord Jesus'*, pg 156, World Library Publications

429 Elie Wiesel *'Night'*, pg 76, Penguin Books

430 Frank Topping *'Wings of the Morning'*, pg 62, Lutterworth Press

433 David Konstant *'Jesus Christ, the Way, the Truth and the Life'*, pg 163, Collins

436 Joe Seremane (of South Africa) *'Lifelines'*, edited by Pamela Searle, Christian Aid, 1987

437 Morris West *'The Shoes of the Fisherman'*, William Heinemann Ltd

438 Peter de Rosa *'Bible Prayer Book for Today'*, pg 91, Collins Fount

441 Cardinal Basil Hume *'To be a Pilgrim'*, pg 49, DLT

442 *'Catechism of the Catholic Church'*, no 2560

443 Thomas à Kempis *'The Imitation of Christ'*

444 Richard Gwyn, OCSO *'The Psalms in Haiku Form'*, Gracewing

445 Cardinal Basil Hume, from a funeral homily he gave

446   Denis Blackledge, SJ *'Loving Lord: Seasons'*, pg 38, Sanctuary Books, Preston

451   Denis Blackledge, SJ *'Loving Lord: Seasons'*, pg 41, Sanctuary Books, Preston

452   G K Chesterton *'The Everlasting Man'*

453   *Revelation 21*[1-7], Good News Bible, copyright of American Bible Society, New York, 1966

454   Palestinian Women of Jerusalem, World Day of Prayer, Commercial Road, Tunbridge Wells, Kent TN1 2RR

457   Gerard Hughes, SJ *'The God of Surprises'*, DLT

458   Rex Chapman *'A Kind of Praying'*, SCM Press

459   Flor McCarthy, SDB *'Sundays and Holy Day Liturgies'*, Cycle B, pg 72, Dominican Publications

460   Anthony Bloom *'School for Prayer'*, pg xi, DLT, 1970

461   Albert Schweitzer *'The Quest of the Historical Jesus'*, A & C Black.
      Permission for inclusion granted by The Albert Schweitzer Institute, Harnden, CT, USA

462   Kathy Galloway *'Love Burning Deep'*, SPCK/Triangle

464   Peter de Rosa *'Emmaus and the broken bread'* from *'Bible Prayer Book for Today'*, pg 66, Collins Fount

465   Edward Farrell *'Gathering the Fragments'*, pg 11, Ave Maria Press, USA

466   Roger Schutz, Prior of Taizé *'Peace of Heart in All Things'*, copyright of A R Mowbray & Co Ltd

467   Edward Farrell *'Gathering the Fragments'*, pg 11, Ave Maria Press, USA

468   Authorship unknown: found among the papers of Damian Lundy FSC, bearing a title of
      'San Damiano, Assisi – Ascension Day'

471   Palestinian Women of Jerusalem, World Day of Prayer, Commercial Road, Tunbridge Wells, Kent TN1 2RR

472   Geoffrey Preston, OP *'God's Way to be Man'*, pg 94, DLT, 1978

474   Lucien Deiss *'Come Lord Jesus'*, pg 162, World Library Publications

475   Francis Brienen *'A Restless Hope'*, United Reformed Church, 86 Tavistock Place, London WC1H 9RT

478   Damian Lundy, FSC *'What's the Point of it All?'*, pg 37, DLT

479   Erasmus (c. 1466-1536) *'Prayers of Erasmus'*, London and Home, 1872

480   Damian Lundy, FSC *'What's the Point of it All?'*, pg 37, DLT

481   Peter de Rosa *'Bible Prayer Book for Today'*, pg 65, Collins Fount

482   Edward Farrell *'Free to be Nothing'*, pg 142, Michael Glazier, Wilmington, USA

485   Karl Rahner, SJ *'Encounters with Silence'*, pg 48, Burns & Oates

486   Edward Farrell *'Gathering the Fragments'*, pg 79, Ave Maria Press, USA

487   Lucien Deiss *'Come Lord Jesus'*, pg 226, World Library Publications

489   Caryll Houselander *'The Reed of God'*, pg 67, Sheed & Ward, 1945

493   Rex Chapman *'A Kind of Praying'*, pg 116, SCM Press

494   Louis Evely *'In His Presence'*, pg 139, Burns & Oates/Herder & Herder, 1970

495   Caryl Micklem *'Contemporary Prayers for Public Worship'*, pg 129, SCM Press

496   Louis Evely *'In His Presence'*, pg 140, Burns & Oates/Herder & Herder, 1970

497   Denis Blackledge, SJ *'Loving Lord: Seasons'*, pg 49, Sanctuary Books, Preston

498   David Adam *'Clouds and Glory: Prayers for the Church Year (A)'*, pg 73, SPCK

501   *'Catechism of the Catholic Church'*, no 2672

502   Caryl Micklem *'Contemporary Prayers'*, SCM Press

503   Lucien Deiss *'Come Lord Jesus'*, pg 181, World Library Publications

504 Karl Rahner, SJ *'Theological Investigations'*, DLT

505 Cardinal Carlo Martini *'Ministers of the Gospel'*, pg 94, St Pauls, 1983

508 Denis Blackledge, SJ *'Loving Lord: Seasons'*, pg 55, Sanctuary Books, Preston

509 Cardinal Jean-Marie Lustiger *'First Steps in Prayer'*, pg 24, Collins Fount

510 Peter de Rosa *'Bible Prayer Book for Today'*, pg 84, Collins Fount

512 Peter de Rosa *'Bible Prayer Book for Today'*, pg 80, Collins Fount

515 St Gregory of Nyssa *'Commentary on the Song of Songs'*

516 Richard Gwyn, OCSO *'The Psalms in Haiku Form'*, Gracewing

517 Edward Farrell *'Gathering the Fragments'*, pg 15, Ave Maria Press, USA

518 Richard Gwyn, OCSO *'The Psalms in Haiku Form'*, Gracewing

519 John O'Donohue *'Eternal Echoes'*, pg 110, Bantam Books

524 Jean Vanier *'Compassion'*, DLT

525 Archbishop William Temple *'A Book of School Worship'*, Macmillan General Books

532 Flann Lynch OFM Cap, Dublin Street, Carlow, Ireland

533 Lucien Deiss *'Come Lord Jesus'*, pg 191, World Library Publications

534 John F X Harriott *'The Tablet'*, 14 Jan 1989, *Periscope*, *'Faith's Central Mystery'*

535 Caryl Micklem *'Contemporary Prayers for Public Worship'*, pg 132, SCM Press

536 Edward Farrell *'Gathering the Fragments'*, pg 55, Ave Maria Press, USA

537 David Adam *'The Open Gate'*, pg 30, Triangle/SPCK

540 Dame Cicely Saunders, Founder of the Hospice Movement

541 Mary Rosenberger *'Sacraments in a Refrigerator'*, Brethren Press, 1451 Dundee Avenue, Elgin, Illinois 60120, USA

542 Peter O'Ryan, in a letter to *'The Tablet'*, 8 June 2002

543 Blaise Pascal, 1623-1662 *'Selected Writings of Blaise Pascal'*, translated by Robert Van de Weyer, Hunt & Thorpe, 1991

545 Rabindranath Tagore (1861-1941) from *'Gintanjali'*, a collection of songs.

546 Mother Teresa *'A Simple Path'*, Ballantine Books, 1995

547 Henri Nouwen *'Bread for the Journey'*, Harper San Francisco, 1997

548 Henri Nouwen *'Life of the Beloved'*, New York, Crossroad, 1992

549 Cardinal Basil Hume, from a funeral homily for a friend

552 Thornton Wilder *'The Bridge of San Luis Rey'* – the last words of the novel

555 Victor Hugo, based on a passage from his *'Toilers of the Sea'*

556 Minnie Louise Haskins – this is repeated from B9 in this volume of Walk In My Presence

557 Henri Nouwen *'Our Greatest Gift: a meditation on dying and caring'*, Hodder & Stoughton, 1994

559 George Appleton *'Journey for a Soul'*, pg 241, Fontana Books, 1974

560 Rabindranath Tagore (1861-1941) from *'Gintanjali'*, a collection of songs.

561 St Teresa of Avila, 1515-1582 *'The Complete Works of St Teresa of Avila'*, translated by Edgar Peers, Sheed & Ward, 1946

562 Luke 2²⁹⁻³¹ from *'The Song of Simeon'* – The *'Nunc Dimittis'*, The Grail

563 St Clare of Assisi, about to die, speaking to herself

566 Nicholas Hutchinson, FSC inspired by texts in Scripture, in the Liturgy, and in the Fathers

567 Attributed to William Penn and also to others; the prayer is not by Bede Jarrett

568 Based on themes from *The Roman Missal*

571 HM Queen Elizabeth II, from her message to British relatives of those killed in New York on 11 September 2001

572 HM Queen Elizabeth, the Queen Mother, on being asked if, after many years of widowhood, her sense of loss eased

574 Michael Walker *'Everyday Prayers'*, The International Bible Reading Association, 1978

575 Leslie D Weatherhead, copyright of William Neill-Hall Ltd

576 Denis Blackledge, SJ *'Loving Lord: Horizons'*, Sanctuary Books, Preston

The Publishers are grateful to the following for permission to include copyright material in this publication.
Albert Schweitzer Institute, Quinnipiac University, Hamden, CT 06518.
A P Watt Ltd, 20 John Street, London WC1P 2DL on behalf of The Grail.
Ave Maria Press, P.O.Box 428, Notre Dame, Indiana 46556-0428.
Bantam, Doubleday Dell, a division of Random House, Inc., 1540 Broadway, New York, NY 10036.
Columba Press, 55a Spruce Avenue, Stillorgan Industrial Park, Blackrock, Co. Dublin.
Continuum International Publishing Group Ltd, The Tower Building, 11 York Road, London SE1 7NX.
Curtis Brown Literary Agents, Haymarket House, 28/29 Haymarket, London SW1Y 4SP for Frank Topping.
Darton, Longman and Todd Ltd, 1 Spencer Court, 140 Wandsworth High Street, London SW18 4JJ.
Dominican Publications, 42 Parnell Square, Dublin 1, Ireland.
Doubleday Publishers, a division of Random House Inc., 1540 Broadway, New York, NY 10036.
Gracewing Ltd, 2 Southern Avenue, Leominster, Herefordshire, HR6 0QF.
HarperCollins Publishers Ltd, 77-85 Fulham Palace Road, Hammersmith,London W6 8JB.
Hodder & Stoughton, 338 Euston Road, London, NW1 3BH.
International Bible Reading Association, 1020 Bristol Road, Selly Oak, Birmingham B29 6LB.
Liturgical Press, St. John's Abbey, P.O. Box 7500, Collegeville, MN 56321-7500.
Lutterworth Press, PO Box 60, Cambridge, CB1 2NT, England.
Paulist Press, 997 Macarthur Blvd., Mahwah, NJ 07430.
Penguin Books Ltd, 80 Strand, London, WC2R 0RL.
Resources for Christian Living, P.O. Box 7000, Allen, Texas, 75013-1305.
Sanctuary Books, 1 Winckley Square, Preston PR1 3JJ.
SCM-Canterbury Press Ltd, 9-17 St Alban's Place, London N1 0NX, UK.
St Paul Publications, Middle Green, Slough SL3 6BS.
Triangle/SPCK, Holy Trinity Church, Marylebone Road, London NW1 4DU.
Veritas Publications, 7/8 Lower Abbey Street, Dublin 1.
Wild Goose Publications, Unit 15, Six Harmony Row, Glasgow G51 3BA.
World Library Publications, 3825 N. Willow Road, Schiller Park, IL 60176.

Locating some prayers and readings by phrases – Vol. 2

A narrow way – 417

At last, all powerful Master – 562

Be born in us, Incarnate Love – 490

Can we recall any occasion? – 504

Christian experience confirms that we can only come to know – 457

Death is nothing at all, I have only slipped away – 554

Descend, Holy Spirit of life! Come down into our hearts – 530

Do not be afraid; I bring you news of great joy – 348

Do not let your love be a sham – 528

Do this in memory of me – 400, 401

Every birth is truly a miracle – 352

Every year, my God, your Church celebrates – 304

Face of God – 346, 349, 353, 510, 553

Father, deepen my conviction that when I am weak, then I am strong – 438

Father, give us the grace to accept the forgiveness – 481

Father, I abandon myself into your hands – 397, 564

Father, I like the abundance implied in the verb, 'to pour' – 512

Father, I thank you for what you have revealed – 317

Father, in sympathising with Christ on his cross – 421

Father, Son and Holy Spirit, I adore you – 380, 532

Father, when I look back on my life – 373

For three long and joyous years we had followed him – 459

Forget, Lord, that it was human hands – 434

From the land of the Resurrection and the cradle of the promise – 471

Go forth, **N**, upon your final journey. Go from this world – 566

Go now; it is quite safe to leave – 563

God, grant me the serenity to accept the things – 406

God of surprises – 475

God our Father, I know that to forgive someone – 378

Grief is the price we pay for love – 571

He did not make the heavens in his image – 515

Help us, O risen Lord, to proclaim your resurrection by – 474

Holy Spirit, who came upon the Virgin Mary – 503

Homeliest home – 484

'How many roads must a man walk down?' – 415

I delight in being able to dip my hand into a basin of holy water – 509

I now see clearly that, if there is any path at all – 485

I once asked a man who knew he was dying what he needed above all – 540

I pray, Lord, that the simplicity of your presence – 349

I said to the man who stood at the gate of the Year – 361, 556

I want to tell you about the Word of Life – 341

I will lift my eyes unto the hills to adore you – 468

If compassion is to be a presence – 524

If God is for us, who is against us? – 430

If Jesus Christ is not true God/Man – 422

If only the bread and wine is changed – 398

In a cave on a windswept Italian mountainside – 347

In the fullness of time, Father – 344

It is easy to believe that God is for us on a sunny day – 430

It is no good caring deeply for people and concealing this – 525

Jesus comes to us as One unknown – 461

Jesus is the face of God – 353

Let us see whether the Spirit has been at work – 504

Lord, come alive within my experience – 458

Lord Jesus Christ, you are the sun that always rises – 479

Lord Jesus, in agony in the Garden of Olives – 428

Lord, may the end of my life be the best part of my life – 544

Lord, we bring our work to your working hands – 395

Index – Vol. 2 (the numbers refer to items, not pages)